CRIMINALISTICS
LABORATORY MANUAL

CRIMINALISTICS LABORATORY MANUAL

The Basics of Forensic Investigation

ELIZABETH ERICKSON

ELSEVIER

AMSTERDAM • BOSTON • HEIDELBERG • LONDON
NEW YORK • OXFORD • PARIS • SAN DIEGO
SAN FRANCISCO • SINGAPORE • SYDNEY • TOKYO

Anderson is an Imprint of Elsevier

Acquiring Editor: Sara Scott
Project Managers: Andre Cuello, Karen East and Kirsty Halterman

Anderson Publishing is an imprint of Elsevier
225 Wyman Street, Waltham, MA 02451, USA

Notices
Knowledge and best practice in this field are constantly changing. As new research and experience broaden our understanding, changes in research methods or professional practices may become necessary. Practitioners and researchers must always rely on their own experience and knowledge in evaluating and using any information or methods described herein. In using such information or methods they should be mindful of their own safety and the safety of others, including parties for whom they have a professional responsibility.

To the fullest extent of the law, neither the Publisher nor the authors, contributors, or editors assume any liability for any injury and/or damage to persons or property as a matter of products liability, negligence or otherwise, or from any use or operation of any methods, products, instructions, or ideas contained in the material herein.

Library of Congress Cataloging-in-Publication Data
Application submitted

British Library Cataloguing-in-Publication Data
A catalogue record for this book is available from the British Library.

ISBN: 978-1-4557-3140-4

For information on all Anderson publications visit our
website at http://store.elsevier.com

Printed in the United States of America
13 14 15 16   10 9 8 7 6 5 4 3 2 1

Working together to grow
libraries in developing countries

www.elsevier.com | www.bookaid.org | www.sabre.org

ELSEVIER   BOOK AID International   Sabre Foundation

DEDICATION

Criminalistics Laboratory Manual is dedicated to the students in the Criminal Investigations program at SUNY Canton. The enthusiasm and endless series of forensic related questions inspired me to design a manual that would assist with processing an entire scene from the crime to the courtroom. Along the way many people were instrumental in making the lab manual a reality, including Gerald Sacca who provided instrumental advice on writing my first book, Di Para who read countless drafts of each chapter and provided lay person advice on understanding the principles of the exercises, Greg Kie who spent many evenings helping me set up scenes and evidence in order to take the perfect photographs, and Dwayne Wisbey and Jennifer Wilson, both former colleagues who supplied technical advice. This book would not have been possible without the support of each and every person in my life...thank you!

CONTENTS

PREFACE

When I worked as a forensic scientist in the crime laboratory, a crime would occur and the lead investigator and crime scene technician would work directly with the various forensic scientists to discuss the case and determine the relevant evidence. The first responding officer would arrive at the scene, causing a chain reaction of personnel and steps that needed to be completed before a case could be presented at trial successfully. There are many people involved in the process, and each contributing party plays an important part from the crime scene to the court trial. This laboratory manual was created to demonstrate the steps from the initial crime scene call to final testimony presented to the jury at a criminal court case.

In higher education, forensic science is a popular course of study, and the majority of forensic science classes are delivered in a laboratory setting using the principles derived from science disciplines, such as chemistry and biology. Forensic science courses have been offered as electives in recent years and are presented in non-laboratory-based settings or instructed fully online. A main component of a forensic science course is the hands-on examination and processing of evidence, but in a non-laboratory or online setting this can be difficult to accomplish.

The *Criminalistics Laboratory Manual: The Basics of Forensic Investigation* was developed to offer forensic science activities that can be completed in a traditional lecture-based classroom or at home for online courses. Each activity requires a limited amount of resources that can be made from household products or office supplies. No chemicals or laboratory equipment is needed to successfully complete each of the 17 labs.

In the forensic science field, most disciplines do not work independently of each other, and for most major cases, many disciplines analyze the evidence. An example would be a homicide involving a firearm. The weapon could be processed for fingerprints, DNA, and/or firearm examination. Each discipline and forensic scientist would work in conjunction to produce results that could be sent to the investigator and used to locate the suspect. The various individuals would work together throughout the evidence processing phase and would reconvene again during the trial to provide expert witness testimony to the jury.

Criminalistics Laboratory Manual: The Basics of Forensic Investigation demonstrates each step of the process, from the initial 911 call to the final questions used for qualification of an expert witness at trial. Each chapter can be completed as a separate entity to further understand the specific forensic science discipline or, if the laboratory manual is completed as a whole, the homicide is explained and a suspect is found. Instruction to complete the material in a traditional classroom environment or in an online course is contained within each chapter for ease of laboratory completion.

The double homicide of William and Jane Ashley was created to incorporate each forensic science discipline with the intention of solving the crime.

You are now acting as a forensic specialist who needs to process the scene and work through each forensic discipline in order to find the culprit. Good luck processing and make sure you solve the case!

DIGITAL ASSETS

Thank you for selecting Anderson Publishing's *Criminalistics Laboratory Manual: The Basics of Forensic Investigation.* To complement the learning experience, we have provided a number of online tools to accompany this edition. Two distinct packages of interactive digital assets are available: one for instructors and one for students.

Please consult your local sales representative with any additional questions.

For the Instructor

Qualified adopters and instructors need to register at this link for access: http://textbooks.elsevier.com/web/manuals.aspx?isbn=9781455731404

- **Instructor's Manual** Additional instructions for how to conduct the lab exercises

For the Student

Students will need to visit this link in order to access the ancillaries given here: http://www.elsevierdirect.com/companion.jsp?ISBN=9781455731404

- **Blank Investigation Forms** For use in exercises
- **Full-Color Image Bank**

INTRODUCTION

THE CRIME

Discovery

On a sunny, warm Sunday evening when daylight still had a few more hours in the sky, Lynette Saunders arrived at her employer's house around 7:00 pm (1900 hours) to walk Mr. and Mrs. Ashley's two dogs. The Sunday night dog walk through the

iStockphoto.

local park had been a ritual for over a year and Lynette often looked forward to seeing Muffin, a small caramel-colored Pekingese, and Gracie, a small light beige Chihuahua. When Lynette arrived at the two-story brown brick townhome she noticed small reddish-brown stains on the front steps, but otherwise nothing was disturbed. When Lynette went to ring the doorbell she noticed the front door was slightly ajar and unlocked. This was extremely unusual, as Mr. and Mrs. Ashley were typically very conscientious about keeping the premise secured.

Case Facts to Date

- 1900 hours
- One person entering scene—Lynette Saunders
- Weather—warm, sunny
- Front door unlocked and slightly open, but no signs of disturbance
- Small reddish brown spots on front step

When Lynette entered the residence she called out to Mr. and Mrs. Ashley, but did not get a response. This was also unusual, as both husband and wife were always home Sunday nights in anticipation of Lynette's scheduled arrival. When Lynette moved into the front hallway, Muffin, the Pekingese dog, came bounding down the front staircase. When Lynette bent down to pick up the dog she noticed reddish-brown stains on both front paws. She immediately assumed the dog had gotten into the kitchen trash and had coffee grounds or dirt on her paws so she took Muffin to the hall bathroom to get cleaned up. After Lynette had Muffin clean, she called for Gracie, the Chihuahua, but no dog appeared. It was a very unusual occurrence that both Gracie and her owners were not coming to greet Lynette at the door. Now concerned and a little curious, Lynette went through the house calling for Gracie; when she arrived in the upstairs hallway she noticed faint reddish-brown paw prints on the expensive Persian carpet. On the double doors leading to the master bedroom there was a clear handprint in the same reddish-brown substance, which Lynette immediately understood was not used coffee grounds from the trash, but was blood. But whose blood and where were Gracie and Mr. and Mrs. Ashley?

Lynette tentatively called for Mr. and Mrs. Ashley and slowly opened the master bedroom door, trying not to touch the blood around the door knob. When the bedroom door was wide open, Lynette called out one more time, but this time it was not for Mr. and Mrs. Ashley or for Gracie. Instead, Lynette started screaming as loud as she could, grabbed Muffin, and ran down the stairs and out the front door.

The 911 Call

Once outside, Lynette fumbled for her cell phone and dialed 911. When the call connected, she choked out what she had seen in the upstairs bedroom and screamed that something terrible had happened to her employers.

The 911 Call Transcript

911 Operator: 911, what is your emergency?

Lynette Saunders: I think something has happened to my employers, Mr. and Mrs. Ashley. There is blood everywhere...oh my god, so much blood.

911 Operator: Ma'am, where are you calling from?

Lynette Saunders: 102 Park Avenue.

911 Operator: Okay, who am I speaking with?

Lynette Saunders: Lynette Saunders, the dog walker. Please, you need to send someone. I think the Ashleys are dead.

911 Operator: Why do you think something has happened?

Lynette Saunders: There is blood in the house and on the master bedroom door.

911 Operator: Did you enter the master bedroom?

Lynette Saunders: I opened the door...so much blood. When I opened the door I saw the Ashleys in the room. They were not moving. I think they are dead.

911 Operator: Alright Lynette, you need to calm down and exit the residence. Stay outside until the police arrive. Someone should be there in 5 minutes.

The Police

Police and medical personnel arrived at the Ashley residence at 7:26 pm (1926 hours) and found Lynette Saunders sitting with a Pekingese dog on the front stoop. Lynette described what she saw in the master bedroom and let the police enter the residence.

Officer O'Donnell and Officer Brown drew their weapons and entered the residence. Officer O'Donnell searched the downstairs looking for any suspects, additional victims, and evidence while Officer Brown went upstairs to check on the reported bodies of Mr. and Mrs. Ashley. Officer Brown saw the bloody handprint on the master bedroom door and drew his weapon in case suspects were still present behind the bedroom door. He slowly pushed back the door and noticed the lights were turned off and all of the windows appeared to be closed. Officer Brown called out to Jane and William Ashley, but did not receive a response. When he turned on his flashlight and scanned the room he noticed bloody footwear impressions on the carpet and blood on the surrounding walls. One body, which appeared to be Jane Ashley, was laying face down on the bed dressed in a cocktail dress and a second body, which appeared to be William Ashley, was laying at the foot of the bed on the floor dressed in a black tuxedo. The only thing missing from the crime scene at the Ashley residence was Gracie, the Chihuahua.

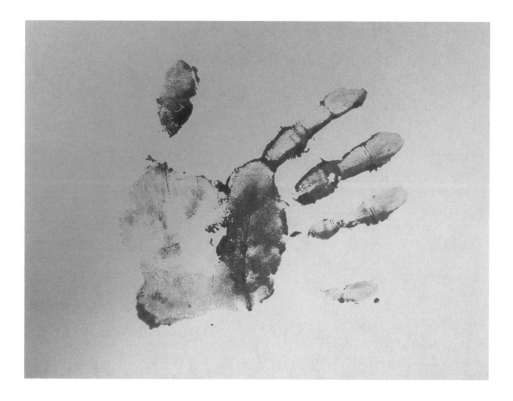

Case Facts to Date

- 1926–1930 hours
- Two officers present at the scene
- Bedroom lights turned off and windows closed
- Two bodies in the master bedroom, one female and one male, assumed to be William and Jane Ashley

Victims

William Ashley

Date of birth—February 20, 1950
Caucasian male, gray hair, brown eyes
No scars, tattoos, and/or birthmarks
Known smoker
Blood type O+

Jane Ashley

Date of birth—May 4, 1951
Caucasian female, brown hair, green eyes
No scars, tattoos, and/or birthmarks
Nonsmoker
Blood type A–

Witnesses

Lynette Saunders

Date of birth—June 18, 1990
Caucasian female, blonde hair, blue eyes
One butterfly tattoo on lower back, no scars, no birthmarks
Nonsmoker
Blood type O–

Police Officers

Officer Melissa O'Donnell

Officer Scott Brown

Suspects

Doug Parsons

Plumber who recently completed work at the Ashley residence
Date of birth—August 11, 1971
Caucasian male, brown hair, brown eyes
Anchor tattoo on right bicep, one scar on left cheek, no birthmarks
Known smoker
Blood type B+

John Lee

Lynette Saunder's boyfriend who sometimes helped with the dog walking
Date of birth—February 20, 1989
Asian male, black hair, brown eyes
No tattoos, scars, or birthmarks
Nonsmoker
Blood type O+

Antonia Sanchez

Jane Ashley's personal assistant
Date of birth—March 9, 1985
Spanish-American female, black hair, gray eyes
One rose tattoo on left hip, no scars, one birthmark on left thigh
Known smoker
Blood type B+

The Interview

Officers O'Donnell and Brown took Lynette Saunders back to the police station to question her about what she did and saw in the house. During the interview, Lynette provided a list of potential people who had access to the Ashley residence during the week.

LABORATORY #1 THE CRIME SCENE SKETCH

LEARNING OBJECTIVES

- Explain the various types of sketches
- Complete a rough sketch
- Complete a final sketch
- Demonstrate measurements within a crime scene
- Measure evidence using triangulation

WHAT YOU WILL LEARN

Laboratory #1, The Crime Scene Sketch, introduces the student to the various search techniques used for processing different types of scenes, such as indoor venues versus outdoor venues. The search techniques are explained with examples and suggestions for when to use one search technique over another. The use of triangulation is explained to measure evidence within a scene, which is also used for the laboratory exercise. Required information for a crime scene sketch is included with information on standard and military time conversions. The chapter ends with a laboratory exercise to show proficiency with creating a rough and final indoor crime scene sketch.

KEY TERMS

demonstrative evidence
elevation sketch
enlarged sketch
exploded sketch
final sketch
location sketch
overview sketch
rough sketch

CASE FILE: 00-123456

After Officers Brown and O'Donnell realized that a double homicide had occurred, detectives, crime scene technicians, and the medical examiner were contacted for further processing of the scene. When the detectives arrived, the entire scene was cordoned off to prevent unnecessary people from entering and exiting in the hopes of preventing contamination. The detectives began to work on assessing the circumstances of the case and recreating the events that led to two deaths by interviewing witnesses, including Lynette Saunders.

While the detectives interviewed witnesses, the crime scene technicians and the medical examiner arrived to collect evidence from the scene. The crime scene technicians began to search the scene to locate possible evidence related to the homicide. The technicians located multiple pieces of evidence and placed yellow photo markers next to each item for future photographs, measurements, and finally collection.

The medical examiner checked each body and made observations about the location of each body and noted any outward signs that could assist with time of death determinations, such as rigor, livor, and algor mortis. Once the evidence was photographed around the body, the medical examiner took possession of the body for transport to the morgue.

Evidence Found at the Scene

The crime scene technicians found the following evidence at the crime scene:

- Multiple fingerprints located around the house and in the master bedroom
- Footwear impressions in blood located in the master bedroom and upstairs hallway
- Footwear impressions located outside the rear entrance to the Ashley residence
- Tool mark impressions on the outside of the rear entrance to the Ashley residence
- Red stains presumed to be blood located on the outside front stoop of the Ashley residence
- One blank pad of paper recovered from the kitchen counter
- Cigarette butts found outside at the rear of the Ashley residence
- One crowbar recovered from the master bedroom
- Two cartridge casings recovered from the master bedroom floor near William Ashley

Cell phone found at the scene.

- Three cartridge casings recovered from the master bedroom floor near the foot of the bed
- Multiple hairs and fibers recovered from locations throughout the master bedroom
- Small piece of glass recovered from the master bedroom carpet
- Glass fragments located in the back hallway of the Ashley residence
- Small plastic bag containing a white powdery substance found on the front hallway floor
- Three empty pill bottles found on the upstairs hallway floor
- One pill bottle containing eight small blue tablets located outside in the bushes of the Ashley residence
- One diamond ring located outside on the ground
- One American Express card located outside on the ground
- One pair of black sunglasses located on the kitchen floor of the Ashley residence
- One cell phone located in the front hallway

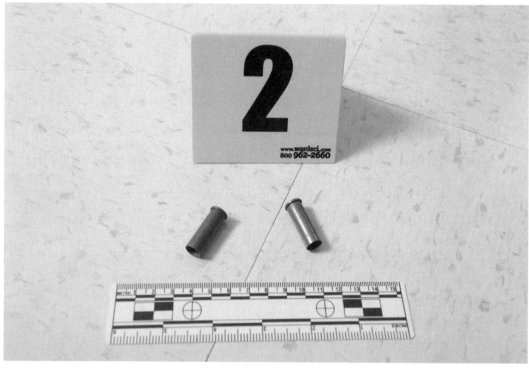

Cartridge casings.

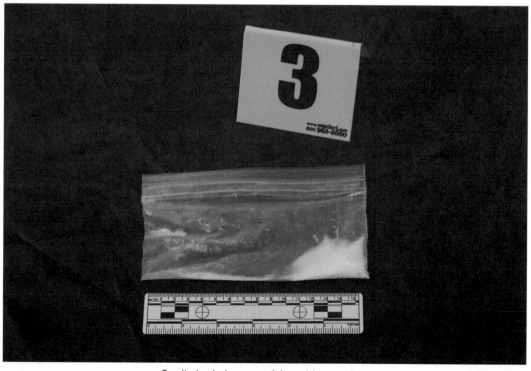

Small plastic bag containing white powder.

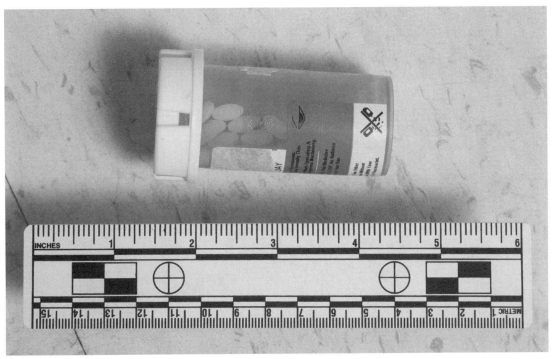

Pill bottle.

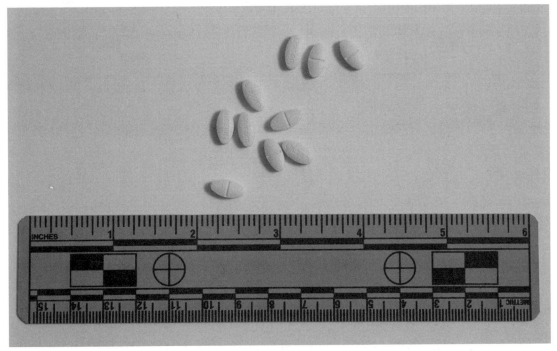

Pills.

American Express card.

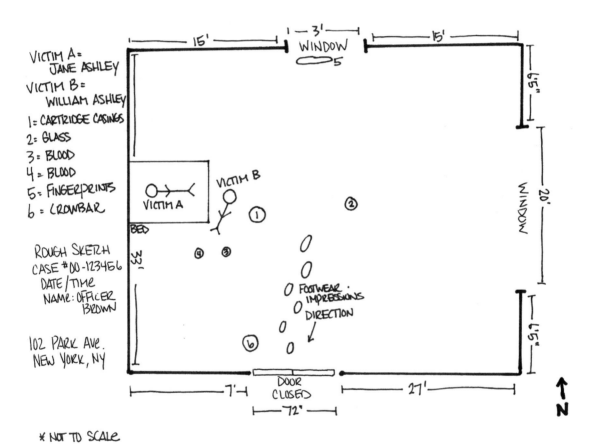

VICTIM A =
  JANE ASHLEY
VICTIM B =
  WILLIAM ASHLEY
1 = CARTRIDGE CASINGS
2 = GLASS
3 = BLOOD
4 = BLOOD
5 = FINGERPRINTS
6 = CROWBAR

ROUGH SKETCH
CASE # 00-123456
DATE / TIME
NAME: OFFICER
       BROWN

102 PARK AVE.
NEW YORK, NY

* NOT TO SCALE

Sketch of where the bodies were located.

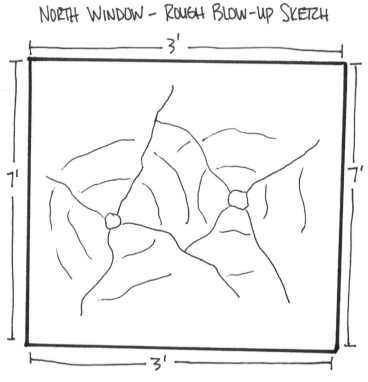

NORTH WINDOW - ROUGH BLOW-UP SKETCH

CASE # 00-123456
DATE / TIME
OFFICER BROWN

102 PARK AVE.
NEW YORK, NY

TWO BULLET HOLES - NORTH MASTER BEDROOM WINDOW

* NOT TO SCALE

North window: Blown-up sketch.

CRIME SCENE SKETCHES

At major crime scenes, including homicides, a crime scene sketch must be made to accompany the pictures and the incident report describing the scene. The sketch is typically drawn by one of the technicians, but with recent technological advances, some departments have the capability of using crime scene sketching software to create a more realistic diagram for court presentation. Depending on the type of scene, multiple sketches would be completed to depict the entire area, specific locations with the body and/or evidence, location of events, etc.

Types of Sketches

Overview Sketch

An overview sketch is sometimes referred to as the crime scene sketch as it is the most common form used at major scenes. The overview sketch depicts the main scene of the case, typically the location with the body or key piece of evidence, and is two dimensional (2D), with the viewer receiving a bird's-eye view of the scene. The overview sketch includes the walls or outer barrier of the scene with permanent and movable items measured and placed appropriately in relation to evidence.

Location Sketch

A location sketch depicts the entire location of the scene and includes the street(s), house location, evidence placement, direction of travel of suspects, and victims. An overall sketch of the scene location can assist with explaining the setting associated with the suspect and victim, such as in the case of gang crimes and territory. An overall sketch of the scene location can also assist the jury with understanding the placement of evidence in a large area, such as in the case of a drive-by shooting with multiple cartridge casings spread out down the street and on the grass.

Investigative Tip

A word processing program can be used to draw the basic perimeter of the crime scene sketch, and symbols can be added to depict furniture, bodies, and evidence.

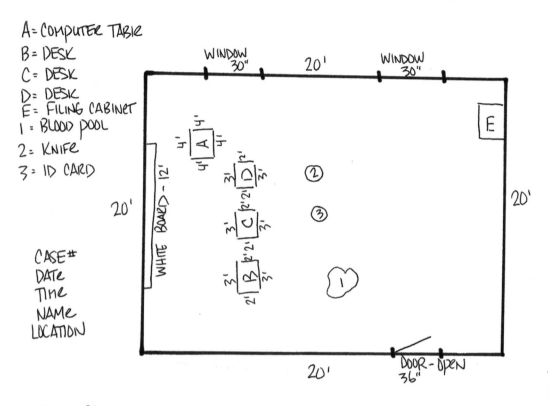

ROUGH OVERVIEW SKETCH

A = COMPUTER TABLE
B = DESK
C = DESK
D = DESK
E = FILING CABINET
1 = BLOOD POOL
2 = KNIFE
3 = ID CARD

CASE #
DATE
TIME
NAME
LOCATION

* NOT TO SCALE

Rough overview sketch.

Elevation Sketch

An elevation sketch depicts the land topography to show higher and lower ground in relation to the scene and pieces of evidence. The elevation sketch is used only at scenes that contain items of evidence scattered over various height differences, usually in an outside setting. The elevation of the land is sketched from a side view to illustrate the difference in height with the evidence and fixed objects measured at the appropriate places.

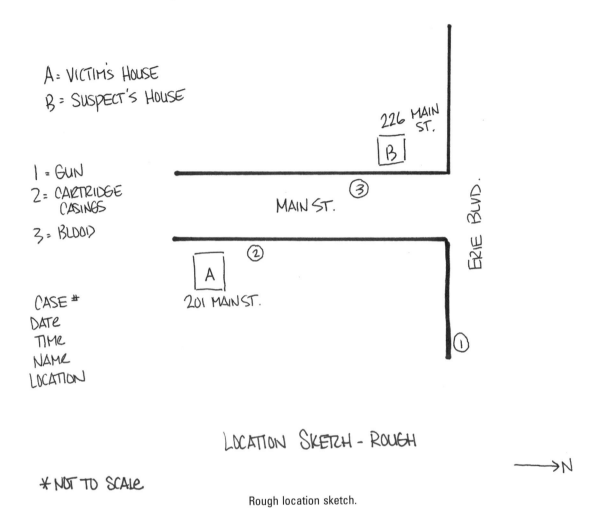

A: VICTIM'S HOUSE
B = SUSPECT'S HOUSE

1 = GUN
2 = CARTRIDGE
    CASINGS
3 = BLOOD

CASE #
DATE
TIME
NAME
LOCATION

226 MAIN ST.

MAIN ST.

ERIE BLVD.

201 MAIN ST.

LOCATION SKETCH - ROUGH

⟶N

* NOT TO SCALE

Rough location sketch.

Exploded Sketch

An exploded sketch is similar to the 2D overview sketch with the addition of all four walls shown flattened. The exploded sketch adds walls to the traditional overview sketch in cases where key pieces of evidence, such as blood spatter and bullet holes, are found located on a wall at a crime scene. The exploded sketch depicts the floor of the crime scene with four separate flattened walls located on each side of the room. In cases where evidence is also contained on the ceiling, an additional overview sketch of the ceiling can be created or a separate sketch of the ceiling can be added to the exploded sketch.

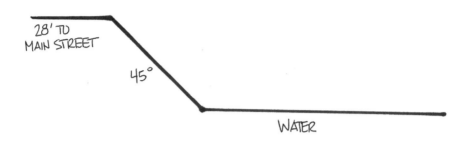

Rough elevation sketch.

Enlarged Sketch

An enlarged sketch depicts one specific area of concentrated evidence at the scene and accompanies an overview or exploded sketch to show more detail. If a crime scene contains blood spatter on one wall within the scene, evidence would be shown on the exploded sketch, but an enlarged sketch would also be used to show the direction of travel and specific measurements associated with the blood stains.

Scene Sketch Requirements

All sketches, regardless of the type, must include basic information about the case and the crime scene so people can reference the material at a later date. Sometimes, additional officers or investigators will work a case at a later date and the sketch is used to orientate the person with the scene. Other times the sketch will be used in court to provide the jurors with a better understanding of the scene and explanation of specific placement for pieces of evidence.

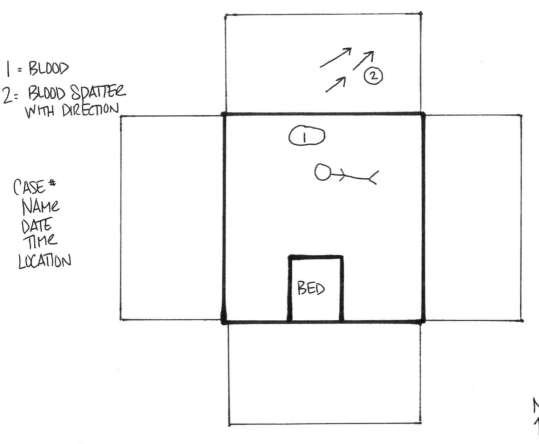

EXPLODED SKETCH- ROUGH

1 = BLOOD

2 = BLOOD SPATTER
   WITH DIRECTION

CASE #
NAME
DATE
TIME
LOCATION

BED

N
↑

* NOT TO SCALE

Rough exploded sketch.

What must be included with the sketch?
- Name of the person completing the sketch
- Date and time the sketch was completed
- Case number (Example: 00-123456)
- Location of the incident
- Direction of north (can be indicated with an arrow and the letter "N")
- Legend showing the evidence (Example: 1 = gun, 2 = cigarette butt, 3 = soda can)

Investigative Tip

Police departments use military time. Example: 1:00 pm = 1300 hours

ENLARGED SKETCH- ROUGH

CASE #
NAME
DATE
LOCATION

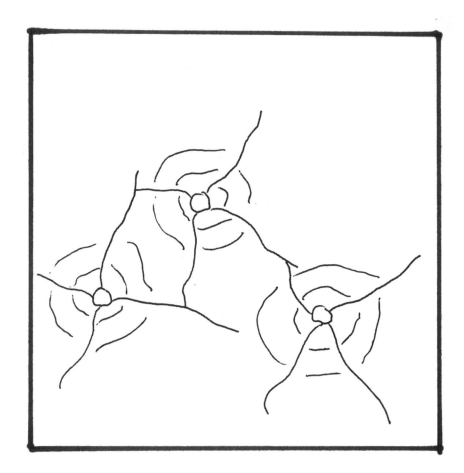

EAST WINDOW
IN
LIVINGROOM

Rough enlarged sketch.

Military Time Conversion Chart

0:00 = 12:00 AM	12:00 = 12:00 PM
1:00 = 1:00 AM	13:00 = 1:00 PM
2:00 = 2:00 AM	14:00 = 2:00 PM
3:00 = 3:00 AM	15:00 = 3:00 PM
4:00 = 4:00 AM	16:00 = 4:00 PM
5:00 = 5:00 AM	17:00 = 5:00 PM
6:00 = 6:00 AM	18:00 = 6:00 PM
7:00 = 7:00 AM	19:00 = 7:00 PM
8:00 = 8:00 AM	20:00 = 8:00 PM
9:00 = 9:00 AM	21:00 = 9:00 PM
10:00 = 10:00 AM	22:00 = 10:00 PM
11:00 = 11:00 AM	23:00 = 11:00 PM

How to Sketch

1. Measure the perimeter of the room including all walls. (Remember this is a 2D sketch and you are looking at the room from above.)
2. Measure the width of all doors and windows.
3. Sketch the location of furniture. (Remember you can draw a chair as a square and label it with a number 1 on the legend.)
4. Sketch the location of all evidence. (Remember you can draw the evidence as a circle with a number in it and label it on the legend.)
5. Measure the evidence using a triangulation method.

Investigative Tip

Fixed objects are something that more than likely will not be moved within the scene at a later date (e.g., window, pillar, staircase).

Ruler.

Measurement of Evidence—Triangulation

There are multiple ways to measure evidence located within a crime scene, but the most common form of measurement is triangulation. Triangulation requires that the evidence be measured from two opposite sides of the scene, forming a triangle. Triangulation is typically used at indoor scenes, but can be used outside as long as fixed objects are selected for the measurement starting points.

Triangulation Example

Item A (gun) is located 8'3" from the SW corner of the room and 9'1" from the SE corner of the room. These measurement lines will always intersect at the location of Item A if the scene needs to be recreated at a later date.

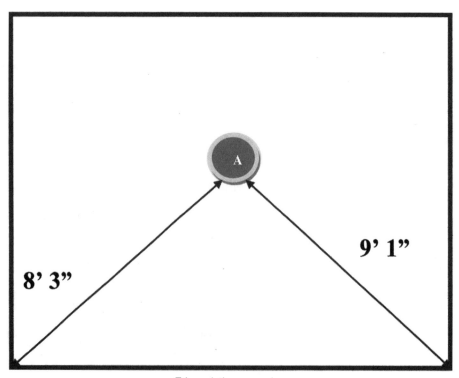

Triangulation example.

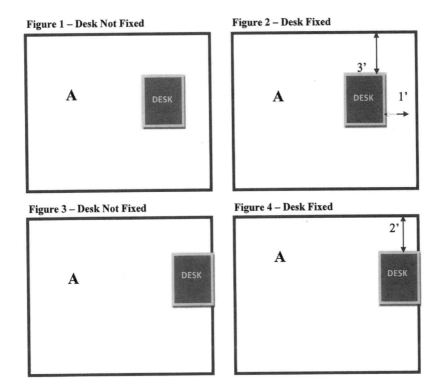

Figure 1 – Desk Not Fixed

Figure 2 – Desk Fixed

Figure 3 – Desk Not Fixed

Figure 4 – Desk Fixed

Evidence must be triangulated to two fixed points. In Figure 1, the desk is located in the east side of the room but is not fixed within the room. If a measurement was completed using the desk as a point of reference without it being fixed you would not be able to recreate the scene at a later date.

How would you fix the desk so you could use it for measuring the evidence?

PRELAB ACTIVITY REVIEW AND PRACTICE

Define the Following Terms

demonstrative evidence
elevation sketch
enlarged sketch
exploded sketch
final sketch
location sketch
overview sketch
rough sketch

Practice Exercise

1 inch = 2.54 cm

1 foot = 12 inches

Example: What would 6 in. convert to in centimeters?

6 in. = 2.54(6) = 15.2 cm

Example: What would 3 ft. 4 in. convert to in centimeters?

3 ft. = 12(3) = 36

36 = 2.54(36 + 4) = 101.6 cm

1. Convert 5 ft. 6 in. into centimeters.
2. Convert 110 cm into feet and inches.

LABORATORY EXERCISE: CRIME SCENE SKETCH

CLASSROOM AND ONLINE INSTRUCTIONS

Classroom Course—If you are completing Laboratory #1 in a classroom setting, use an indoor classroom with at least three desks or workstations to complete the crime scene sketch. The room may not have a window, but you can substitute items, such as a white board or chalkboard, for the window.

Online Course—If you are completing Laboratory #1 in an online course, use an indoor, enclosed room with at least three pieces of furniture to complete the crime scene sketch. The room should have at least one window and one door to highlight all aspects of the sketch.

Materials Needed

- Graph paper
- Ruler or scale
- Writing utensil (preferably a pencil for the rough sketch and a pen for the final sketch)
- Three items that can be used as evidence

The Exercise

1. Using graph paper, create one overview sketch of an indoor scene. Make sure to measure all four sides of the room, including doors and windows.
2. Select three pieces of evidence to be used in your scene and place them around the room. Be creative!
3. Include a legend.

4. Include the required information on the sketch.
   - Case Number 00-123456
   - Date/time
   - Name of person completing the sketch
   - Location
5. Measure the three pieces of evidence using the triangulation system of measurement.
6. Using the incident report included in the appendix, complete one report explaining your crime scene sketch and the scene.

LABORATORY #2 PHOTOGRAPHY

CHAPTER OUTLINE

2.1 **Photography**

2.2 **Laboratory Exercise: Photography**

LEARNING OBJECTIVES

- Understand the difference between traditional and digital photography
- Explain the three types of photographic evidence (overview, midrange, and close-up)
- Demonstrate the three types of photographic evidence
- Comprehend the crime scene forms associated with photographic evidence

WHAT YOU WILL LEARN

Laboratory #2, Photography, introduces the student to various techniques for accomplishing crime scene photographs at both indoor and outdoor scenes. The three main types of photographic evidence, including overview, midrange, and close-up images, are described with examples. The use of filling the frame, a tripod, and a scale with case information is discussed to address the importance of each item for inclusion at trial. The chapter ends with a laboratory exercise to show proficiency with completing photographs of a crime scene and completion of required paperwork.

KEY TERMS

close-up picture
digital photography
fixed point
midrange picture
overview picture
scale
traditional photography

One diamond ring located outside the Ashley residence.

CASE FILE 00-123456

The first responding officers and the investigators contacted the crime scene unit to process the scene for possible evidence. During the crime scene processing, the evidence technicians flagged evidence associated with the double homicide of William and Jane Ashley. Each piece of evidence was documented through photography as a close-up image with a scale. The photographs could then be used for courtroom presentations and for forensic scientists inquiring about the position or location of items. Two specific pieces of evidence, a key fob and a diamond ring, were selected as key pieces of evidence to help the investigators possibly determine a suspect.

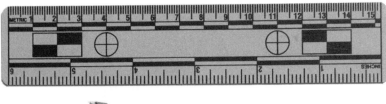

One key fob and keys located on the front hallway floor.

PHOTOGRAPHY

Introduction

At crime scenes, individuals will take pictures to document the scene. The photographs can be used later in the case to refresh the memory of the investigator or as demonstrative evidence to show the jury the relation between the victim and the evidence. In the past, police departments always used traditional photography, which included print film, negatives, and a darkroom for processing. According to the Scientific Working Group on Imaging Technology, digital photography can now be used, as long as the images and the camera abide by the national guidelines.

Types of Investigative Photography

Overview or Establishment

An overview or establishment image shows the entire location of the incident and a broad perspective of the scene. Typically, the overview image will show the direction of travel of the suspect from the exterior of the scene through the interior. The establishment image will show the location of the scene in relation to other fixed items nearby, such as a street sign or nearest intersection.

For example, a scene occurring inside of a classroom would have overview or establishment images depicting the entrance(s) to the campus and roads leading to the building. Once the photographer arrives at the building, images would be taken of the exterior of the building and follow through the door and hallways leading to the entrance to the scene.

The Three Types of Photography

- Overview or establishment
- Midrange
- Close-Up

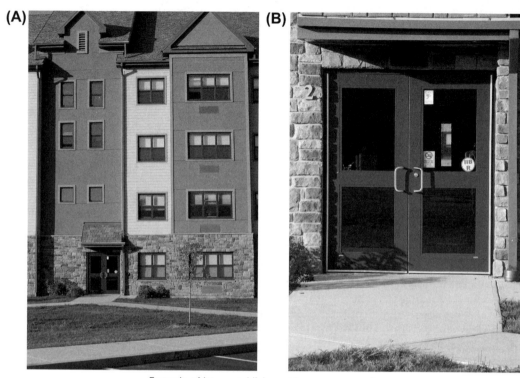

Example of how establishment images are used.

Midrange

A midrange image shows the evidence and/or victim in relation to the scene. The evidence and/or body must be captured with a fixed object in a room. The image can contain more than one piece of evidence in relation to a fixed item. There is no limit to the amount of pictures you should have of a scene, but the rule of thumb is that it is better to have too many pictures than too few.

For example, a scene occurring inside of a classroom would have images of each piece of evidence in relation to something fixed. A window, door, and permanent desk could be used as fixed objects.

Close-Up

A close-up image shows the evidence and fills the frame of the camera. The camera must be parallel to the piece of evidence or the surface that the evidence is on, which is why many departments use a tripod to take pictures. The close-up image of the

Example of a midrange photograph.

evidence should always contain a scale to depict the actual or true size of the image. Sometimes one photograph with a scale and one photograph without a scale are taken, but the image with the scale will be needed for comparison purposes later on.

Example: A scene occurring inside of the classroom where the suspect left a backpack would have a close-up image of the backpack with a scale to show the size of the item.

Things to Keep in Mind While Taking Photographs

Fill the Frame

When taking a picture of an item close up, you must try to fill the frame of the image with the evidence. This means that when you look at the image through the viewfinder you should see the entire piece of evidence filling the screen completely. There should be little to no extra space in the image. By filling the frame,

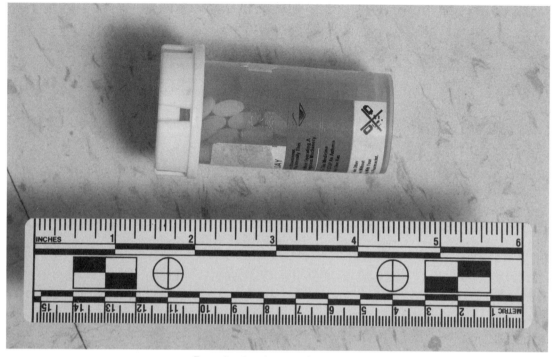

Example of a close-up photograph.

you will have the closest possible image of the evidence for later comparisons.

Use of a Scale

Each image should have a scale or measurement device visible in the picture in relation to the piece of evidence for later 1:1 or true sizing of the photograph. The scale will assist in sizing the photograph later on before a comparison can be completed. An example of this would be a photograph of a footwear impression taken at a crime scene that would appear small if printed on 4×6 paper, but once sized would be 1:1 and would need 11×17 paper to depict the actual size.

The scale does not have to be a traditional ruler but can be any form of scale that shows at least one unit of measurement. You do not need to capture the entire scale in the image, but you do need to have one unit of measurement visible for resizing later on.

The scale must contain information regarding the case and the information must be visible in each image. In the past when investigators used traditional photography, such as 35mm, the first image on the roll would be the crime scene information, as

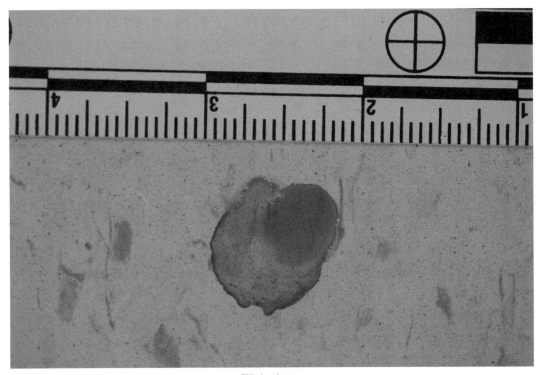

Fill the frame.

Ruler to show scale.

all of the negatives would be stored together. With the advent of digital photography, however, only certain images might be needed for comparisons; therefore, each photograph must contain the case information. You should at a minimum include the case number, the photographer's initials, and the date/time.

Tripod

Whenever possible a tripod should be used in order to guarantee that a parallel image of the evidence is captured. In some

Scale with case information.

instances, such as footwear and tire impressions, a tripod must be used at the scene as the images cannot be used for comparison purposes if the image cannot be sized properly back in the crime laboratory. If a photographer completes a series of photographs and the images are not parallel to the evidence, a true size cannot be obtained.

PRELAB ACTIVITY REVIEW AND PRACTICE
Define the Following Terms

close-up picture
digital photography
fixed point
midrange picture
overview picture
scale
traditional photography

Practice Exercise

Take some practice pictures to get acquainted with the camera. Practice taking pictures using different objects as evidence and using different levels of lights. If you are working in dark or limited light conditions, you can always use an alternate light source or a flashlight to provide side lighting.

Use of a tripod to photograph evidence.

2.2

LABORATORY EXERCISE: PHOTOGRAPHY

CLASSROOM AND ONLINE INSTRUCTIONS

Classroom Course—If you are completing Laboratory #2 in a classroom setting, you can use a digital camera with a minimum of eight megapixels and remove the camera card for submission to the instructor. You can also download the images from the camera card to your computer. If you only have access to one camera per class, each student can use a different camera card.

Online Course—If you are completing Laboratory #2 in an online course, you can use a digital camera with a minimum of eight megapixels and upload the photographs to your computer. The photographs can be saved in a folder titled "laboratory #2" and emailed or uploaded to the online course shell.

Materials

- Digital camera (minimum eight megapixels)
- Pen
- Ruler or scale
- Three items that can be used for evidence

The Exercise

1. View the sample photography log to see the proper information that must be contained in the form. Using the blank photography log located in the appendix, complete a photography log for all scene photographs. Use the case information and describe each image in the appropriate sections.
2. Assume that a crime has occurred in your classroom. Go outside the building and take a series of overview and establishment pictures to describe the scene through photographs.

Remember to work your way through from the outside of the building to the inside where the crime is located.

3. Select at least three pieces of evidence and place them throughout your scene. Complete midrange photographs of the three pieces of evidence using fixed objects in the classroom.

4. Using the same three pieces of evidence, complete close-up images using a scale and remember to fill the frame with the item. Make sure the scale includes the case information (00-123456).

SAMPLE PHOTO LOG
Case # _____
Investigator _____

Date/Time	Photo #	Type Photo	Photo Depicts
JUNE 25, 2012 1930 HOURS	1	OVERVIEW	OUTSIDE OF RESIDENCE (ADDRESS)
JUNE 25, 2012 1931 HOURS	2	MIDRANGE	CIGARETTE BUTT (LABELED ITEM #1)
JUNE 25, 2012 1932 HOURS	3	CLOSE-UP	CIGARETTE BUTT (LABELED ITEM #1)

Sample photo log.

LABORATORY #3 EVIDENCE COLLECTION

CHAPTER OUTLINE

3.1 Evidence Collection
3.2 Laboratory Exercise: Evidence Packaging

LEARNING OBJECTIVES

- Understand the various search techniques for indoor and outdoor scenes
- Describe items for submission as evidence
- Comprehend the crime scene forms for evidence collection

WHAT YOU WILL LEARN

Laboratory #3, Evidence Collection, introduces the student to various search techniques used for both indoor and outdoor scenes. Evidence submission and chain of custody forms are included with completed forms to use as a guide. The need for descriptions of evidence is explained with examples on how to uncover possible evidence at crime scenes. The chapter ends with a laboratory exercise to show proficiency with completing the required paperwork for evidence collection, evidence packaging, and chain of custody.

KEY TERMS

chain of custody
grid search
lane search
spiral search
zone search

CASE FILE 00-123456

The police arrived at the scene in response to the 911 call placed by Lynette Saunders, a dog walker for the Ashley family, and found two deceased individuals in the master bedroom. The two victims were presumed to be William and Jane Ashley, the owners of the residence. The first responding officers contacted detectives and crime scene technicians to further investigate the crime and process the scene.

The Ashley residence was fully processed for potential evidence associated with the double homicide. The crime scene technicians flagged evidence after completing a full search of both the inside and the outside of the scene, and the photography of each piece of evidence has been completed.

For review, the crime scene technicians found the following evidence at the crime scene:

- Multiple fingerprints located around the house and in the master bedroom
- Footwear impressions in blood located in the master bedroom and upstairs hallway
- Footwear impressions located outside the rear entrance to the Ashley residence
- Tool mark impressions on the outside of the rear entrance to the Ashley residence
- Red stains presumed to be blood located on the outside front stoop of the Ashley residence
- One blank pad of paper recovered from the kitchen counter
- Cigarette butts found outside at the rear of the Ashley residence
- One crowbar recovered from the master bedroom
- Two cartridge casings recovered from the master bedroom floor
- Multiple hairs and fibers recovered from locations throughout the master bedroom
- Small piece of glass recovered from the master bedroom carpet
- Glass fragments located in the back hallway of the Ashley residence
- Small plastic bag containing a white powdery substance found in the front hallway floor
- Three empty pill bottles found on the upstairs hallway floor
- One pill bottle containing eight small white tablets located outside in the bushes of the Ashley residence
- One cell phone found in the hallway.

Examples of evidence recovered at the Ashley homicide:

Sunglasses.

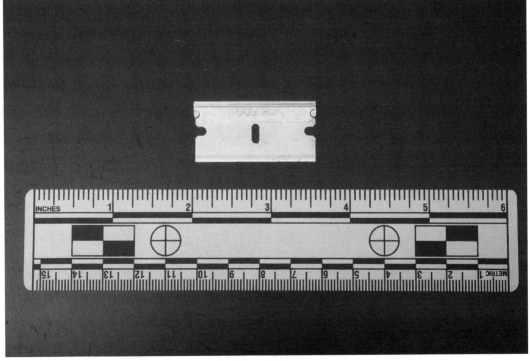

Razor blade.

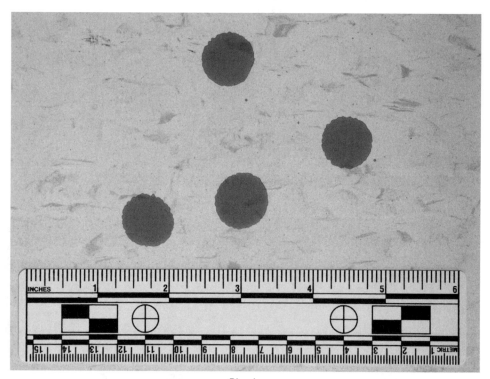

Blood.

EVIDENCE COLLECTION FORM		Case # 00-123456		

TYPE OF CRIME HOMICIDE		DATE / TIME DATE/TIME	REPORT COMPLETED BY YOUR NAME	

PROPERTY STATUS:

X Evidence   □ Recovered   □ Stolen   □ Found   □ Safekeeping   □ Hold (Unit):   □ Other:

Name (If Known)		Sex Race DOB	Address	Phone
Victim: JANE ASHLEY		FEMALE, CAUC., DOB – UNK	LIST ADDRESS OF INCIDENT	PHONE – UNK.
Suspect: UNKNOWN		UNKNOWN	UNKNOWN	UNKNOWN

Item Number	Quantity	Describe Items (Use as much detail as possible)
1	1	ONE EMPTY MARLBORO CIGARETTE PACKAGE
2	1	ONE BLUE BIC LIGHTER
3	2	TWO S&W 9MM CARTRIDGE CASINGS
4	1	ONE CLEAR PLASTIC BAG CONTAINING A WHITE POWDERY SUBSTANCE

Place the Item Number(s) From Above to designate the Examination Requested: Check box if additional items are on an additional form: □

Document Examination	Drug Chemistry 4	Digital Evidence	Toxicology
Tool marks	Hairs and Fibers	Fingerprints 1, 2, 4	Footwear / Tire Impressions
Glass	Biology (Blood Typing, DNA)	Documents	Other (FIREARMS) 3

Narrative/Notes:

Evidence collection form.

CHAIN OF CUSTODY FORM				CASE # 00-123456		
Chain of Custody						
ITEM NUMBER	QUANTITY	PERSON WHO COLLECTED EVIDENCE:	WHERE EVIDENCE WAS DELIVERED TO:		DATE	TIME
1-4	5	OFFICER BROWN	POLICE DEPARTMENT EVIDENCE LOCKER		DATE	TIME
ADDITIONAL CASE INFORMATION						

Chain of custody form.

EVIDENCE COLLECTION

Evidence located at the crime scene must first be uncovered using search techniques and then flagged for photography. Once the midrange and close-up images of the evidence have been completed, the evidence technician can collect the items for proper packaging and submission to an evidence storage locker or the forensic laboratory.

Various search techniques are used depending on the type of scene, such as whether the crime scene is located inside or outside. A line search can be used with one or more crime scene technicians where each person walks shoulder to shoulder in a straight line covering either a short or a long distance. A line or

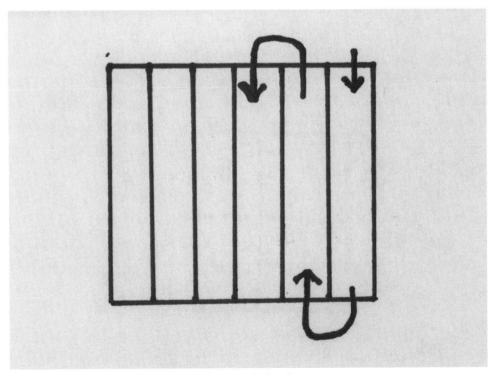

Line search sketch.

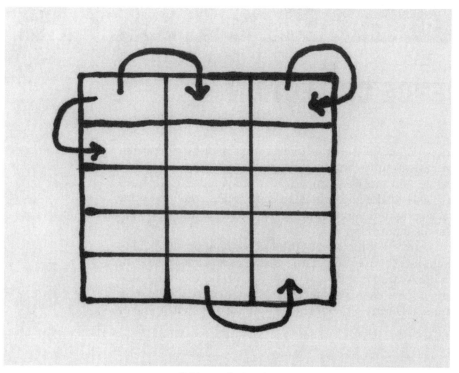

Grid search sketch.

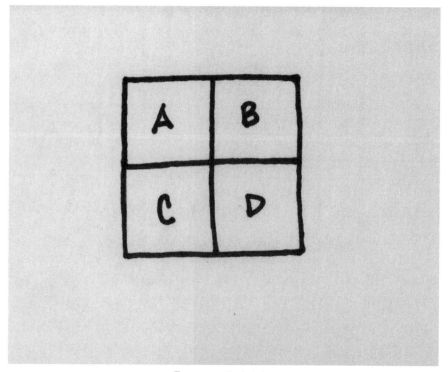

Zone search sketch.

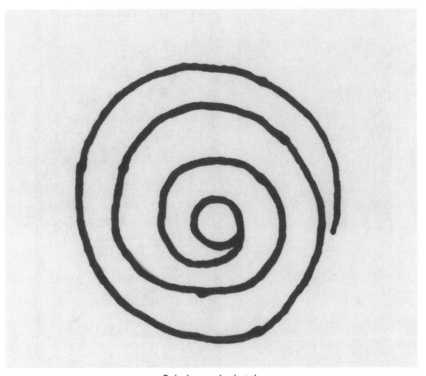

Spiral search sketch.

strip search covers the territory of the crime scene once as each individual walks the entire length of the scene.

A grid search is a double line search where individuals walk the entire length of a scene twice, moving north to south and then east to west. A benefit of the grid search is that the area is searched twice, which can be a more thorough method to locate minute or trace evidence in an outdoor scene.

A zone search divides the scene into multiple quadrants, which allows one individual to apply a search technique to a smaller area. The zone search method works well for large outdoor scenes that may have an abundance of evidence or victims.

A spiral search works either from the outside of the crime scene perimeter to the center or from the center of the scene to the outside perimeter. The individual searches the scene in a spiral fashion; a downside to this search technique is that evidence can be missed if the person does not overlap each circling of the scene.

The evidence must be collected and packaged properly to prevent contamination and later exclusion from court. Each piece

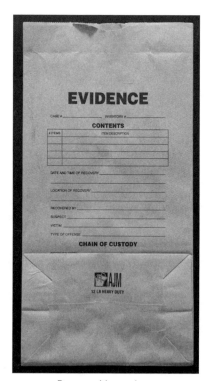

Paper evidence bag.

of evidence must be packaged separately depending on the type of evidence and labeled with a description of the item and initials of the crime scene technician sealing the package. Most types of evidence can be secured using a paper bag, which allows the item to breath and not retain moisture, which can cause mold and mildew to grow. Some types of evidence can be secured using a plastic bag, as the material within the bag should remain visible so damage does not occur during storage. Sharp or breakable evidence can be secured using a box and tie downs to prevent movement.

Once the evidence is secure in the packaging, the bag, box, or tube must be sealed to prevent contamination and a chain of custody form must be completed to track the people who handle the evidence from the crime scene to court. Evidence packaging must be sealed using tape or a heat sealer, and information pertaining to the evidence technician must be written over the seal. The initials of the investigator or evidence technician, the date, and the time of evidence collection are written in permanent marker across the seal to ensure the chain of custody.

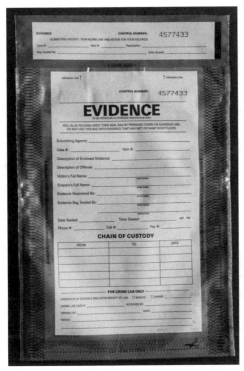

Plastic evidence bag.

Finally, the packaged evidence must be listed on an evidence submission form and chain of custody document before it can be submitted to a police department evidence locker or the forensic laboratory for further processing. The evidence must be documented properly and described accurately on the paperwork. It is up to the investigator when requesting forensic evidence processing at the crime laboratory to select what needs to be documented, such as latent prints, DNA, or footwear.

PRELAB ACTIVITY REVIEW AND PRACTICE

Define the Following Terms

chain of custody
grid search

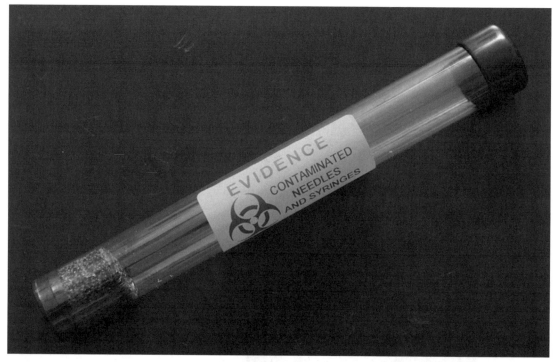

Evidence tube.

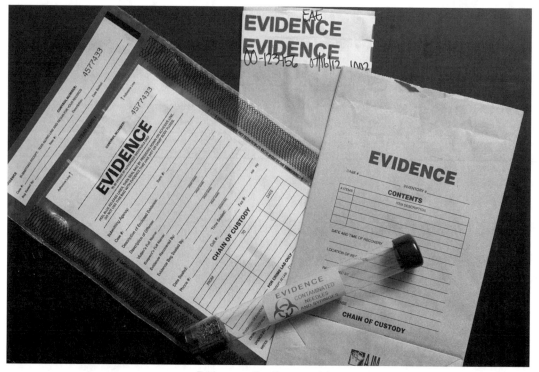

Evidence collection materials.

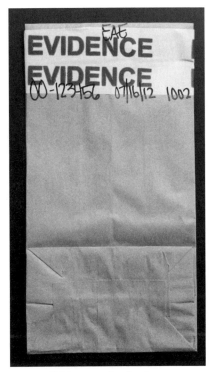

Evidence collection bag.

lane search
spiral search
zone search

Practice Exercise

Select three pieces of evidence recovered at the Ashley residence and practice describing the evidence so another classmate can visualize it. The description on the submission form will assist the investigator with remembering the evidence at a later date, such as during court testimony, and will assist with descriptions during the trial.

3.2

LABORATORY EXERCISE: EVIDENCE PACKAGING

CLASSROOM AND ONLINE INSTRUCTIONS

Classroom Course—If you are completing Laboratory #3 in a classroom setting, use three pieces of evidence from around the classroom. Pretend that a crime has taken place, such as a theft of a backpack, and select pieces of evidence that could be associated with this type of crime. Because you are inside at a classroom crime scene setting, make sure you practice the appropriate search technique.

Online Course—If you are completing Laboratory #3 in an online course, use three pieces of evidence from around the house. Pretend that a crime has taken place, such as a burglary, and select pieces of evidence that could be associated with this type of crime. You can also practice the search techniques associated with both an indoor and an outdoor setting.

Materials Needed

- Pen
- Three items that can be used as evidence

The Exercise

1. Select three pieces of evidence (these can be the same pieces of evidence used during the photography lab)—be creative!
2. Using the blank evidence submission form located in the appendix, complete one submission form and describe each piece of evidence accurately and select the forensic science discipline requests.
3. Using the blank chain of custody form located in the appendix, complete one chain of custody form in order to secure and store the evidence accurately for future analysis.

4

LABORATORY #4 AUTOPSY/ WOUND DOCUMENTATION

CHAPTER OUTLINE

4.1 Autopsy Documentation

4.2 Laboratory Exercise: Autopsy and Wound Documentation

LEARNING OBJECTIVES

- Understand the difference between the medical examiner and the coroner system

- Explain the cause of death, manner of death, and mechanism of death

- Understand the autopsy process

- Demonstrate descriptions used during the autopsy process to identify an individual or a wound

- Comprehend the forms used at an autopsy

WHAT YOU WILL LEARN

Laboratory #4, Autopsy/Wound Documentation, introduces the student to medical examiner and coroner systems in the United States. Cause of death, manner of death, and mechanism of death are explained to demonstrate how each category can be used to assist the investigator with a death investigation. The forms used during the autopsy to describe identifying characteristics and wound orientation are included with completed samples to use as a reference. The chapter ends with a laboratory exercise to show proficiency with completing an autopsy wound documentation form and including proper descriptions of identifying characteristics.

KEY TERMS

autopsy

cause of death

coroner

manner of death

mechanism of death
medical examiner

CASE FILE 00-123456

The medical examiner completed the autopsies for both William and Jane Ashley. The medical examiner included a detailed wound description form to identify entry/exit wounds for ballistics and blunt force trauma injuries. After the autopsy was complete, an autopsy report for both victims was generated to document the cause and manner of death, which was ruled a homicide. It was determined that both William and Jane Ashley had been dead for around 18 hours, placing the time of death between 11:00 pm and 3:00 am the evening before.

Autopsy Report—William Ashley
00-123456

Based on the circumstances surrounding the death as currently known, review of available medical history and records, autopsy findings, and toxicologic analysis, the death of William Ashley, to a reasonable degree of medical certainty, is attributed to exsanguination from contributory conditions of gunshot wounds. The manner of death is homicide.

Circumstances of Death

The decedent was a 62-year-old Caucasian male with a medical history significant for high blood pressure. He was found by first responding Officer Brown. He was pronounced dead at 102 Park Avenue, New York, New York.

Evidence of Injury

The posterior side of the torso has two visible wounds associated with gunshot wounds assumed to be entrance wounds. Based on the characteristics of the wounds, it is assumed that the weapon was within 8—10 inches from the skin surface. The appearance of stippling and gunshot residue (GSR) is visible on the clothing of the decedent with a small amount of burns located on the skin around the wound sites.

The anterior side of the torso has one visible wound associated with a gunshot wound and is assumed to be the exit wound. No other visible wounds appear on the anterior side of the body.

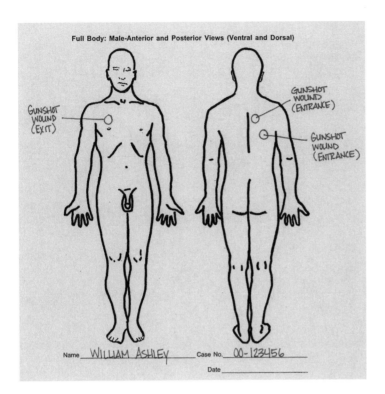

Autopsy Report—Jane Ashley
00-123456

Based on the circumstances surrounding the death as currently known, review of available medical history and records, autopsy findings, and toxicologic analysis, the death of Jane Ashley, to a reasonable degree of medical certainty, is attributed to exsanguination from contributory conditions of blunt force trauma to the head. The manner of death is homicide.

Circumstances of Death

The decedent was a 61-year-old Caucasian female with a medical history significant for anxiety treatment and borderline diabetes. She was found by first responding Officer Brown. She was pronounced dead at 102 Park Avenue, New York, New York.

Evidence of Injury

The head and skull of the decedent have three visible wound sites with two distinct impressions per wound, which could be consistent with either a hammer or a small crowbar. Based on the characteristics of the wounds and the cracks resonating through the skull, the wound located on the posterior side of the skull was the first contact.

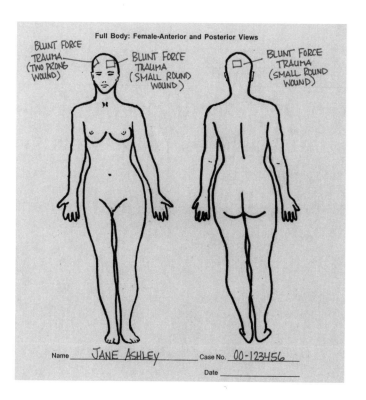

Full Body: Female-Anterior and Posterior Views

BLUNT FORCE TRAUMA (TWO PRONG WOUND)

BLUNT FORCE TRAUMA (SMALL ROUND WOUND)

BLUNT FORCE TRAUMA (SMALL ROUND WOUND)

Name JANE ASHLEY

Case No. 00-123456

Date _____

AUTOPSY DOCUMENTATION

The medical examiner (ME) is the medical professional responsible for conducting an autopsy and determining the cause, manner, and mechanism of death. A medical investigator is assigned to the case and arrives at the scene to take possession of the body for transportation to the morgue. The first step at the medical examiner's office requires information from the exterior of the body to be documented on a wound identification form. The second step is to collect any additional evidence that was not retrieved at the initial crime scene. This can include fingerprints of the deceased, fingernail scrapings, trace evidence collection, sexual assault kit completion, and additional photographs of identifying characteristics and the wounds. The third step is for the ME to complete an autopsy to determine the cause, manner, and mechanism of death. During the autopsy, photographs of the wounds can be completed to track the path of a knife or bullet through the body. Finally, when the autopsy is complete, the body can be released to the family for burial or cremation. Evidence gathered from the autopsy is then sent to the respective forensic science units for further evaluation. Once all of the information and results have been generated, the ME can issue the death certificate and make a determination on the cause of death and manner of death.

The cause of death is the reason, whether it is injury or illness, that led to the subsequent death of the individual. The manner of death is the way in which the actual cause of death happened and is divided into four categories: natural, accidental, suicidal, and homicidal. Natural death occurs without an outside force and, in some cases, can be expected when the person is under the care of a physician, such as death due to cancer. Accidental death is unexpected and, in some cases, can be staged to cover up an actual crime. Suicidal death can have consistencies with homicidal death, but the evidence uncovered during the autopsy links to distance determinations and angles of bruising consistent with self-inflicted wounds. Homicidal death is an unexpected form of manner of death, which requires a full investigation and autopsy to determine additional information that can be used during the investigation.

Investigative Tip

Some jurisdictions in the United States also have a coroner system in which an individual is voted into the office of coroner by the public.

PRELAB ACTIVITY REVIEW AND PRACTICE
Define the Following Terms

autopsy
cause of death
coroner
manner of death
mechanism of death
medical examiner

Practice Exercise

Using the blank autopsy wound diagram located in the appendix, complete a form and describe any visible characteristics on the exterior of your own body. Include any tattoos, birthmarks, scars, etc. that could be used as a visual identification. Also include any cuts, bruises, or marks that could be associated with a trauma. Label all identifying characteristics on the form and include measurements for wounds.

LABORATORY EXERCISE: AUTOPSY AND WOUND DOCUMENTATION

CLASSROOM AND ONLINE INSTRUCTIONS

This laboratory exercise can be performed the same way in both a classroom and online.

Materials Needed

Pen or marker to describe the wounds

The Exercise

1. Using the picture shown below from the autopsy, describe in detail any identifying characteristics from the body and describe the wounds on the blank autopsy diagram form located in the appendix at the end of the book.

2. Using the pictures labeled A–E shown below, describe the wounds in detail. Remember to include the color, size, shape, and location of each wound. The more detail you can provide for the case file the better, as the wound on a live victim will heal over time and the wound on a deceased individual will be inaccessible once the body is released to the family.

Investigative Tip

Identifying characteristics are unique items on the body that can assist in the identification process and can be tattoos, scars, birthmarks, and/or body piercings.

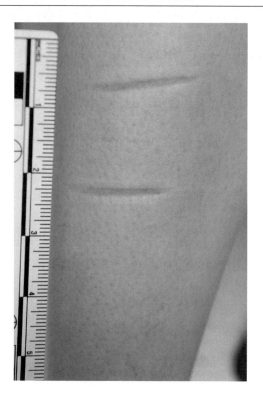

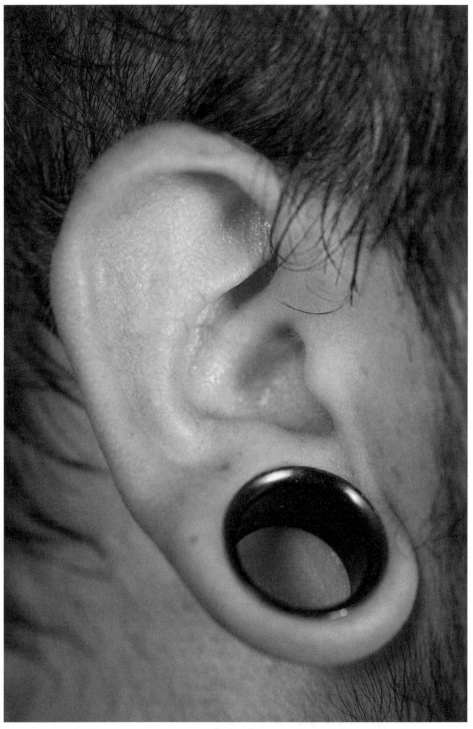

Image A.

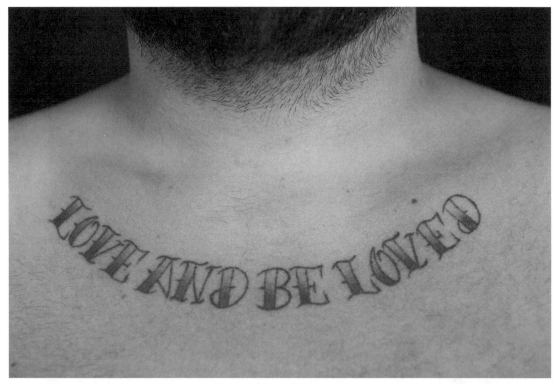

Image B.

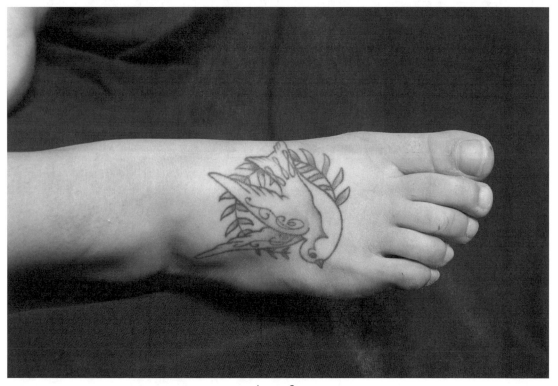

Image C.

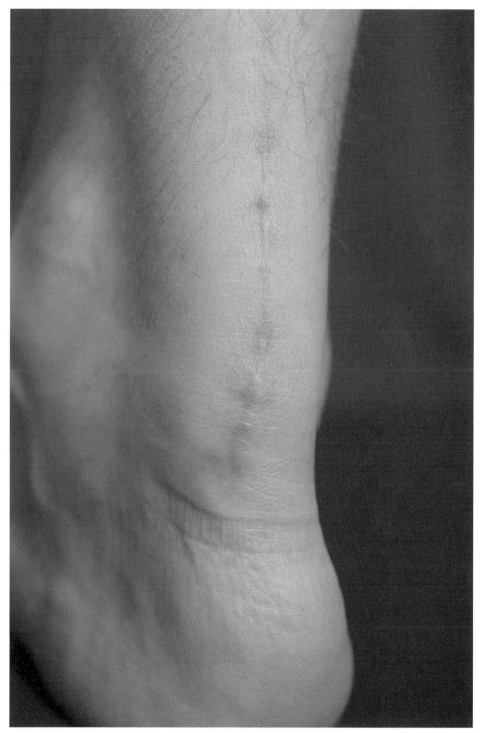

Image D.

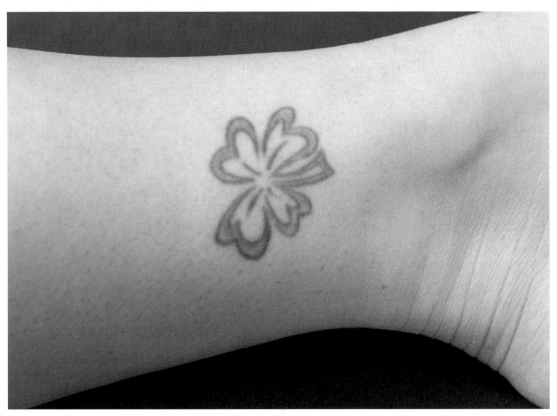

Image E.

5

LABORATORY #5 FINGERPRINT PROCESSING

CHAPTER OUTLINE
5.1 Introduction to Fingerprints
5.2 Laboratory Exercise: Fingerprint Processing

LEARNING OBJECTIVES
- Understand the three categories of fingerprint patterns
- Identify fingerprint patterns
- Explain the three types of fingerprint evidence (latent, patent, and plastic)
- Demonstrate fingerprint processing techniques
- Comprehend the forms used for collection and packaging of fingerprint-related evidence

WHAT YOU WILL LEARN

Laboratory #5, Fingerprint Processing, introduces the student to the three categories of fingerprint evidence, including latent, patent, and plastic prints. Techniques for processing the three categories are highlighted with emphasis placed on fingerprint powdering for latent impressions. The three categories of fingerprint patterns are explained with images to distinguish the differences in definitions. The chapter ends with a laboratory exercise to show proficiency with powdering evidence for fingerprint development and completion of required evidence processing and submission paperwork.

KEY TERMS
arch
latent print
loop
patent print
plastic print
whorl

CASE FILE 00-123456: FINGERPRINT PROCESSING

The police investigators and crime scene technicians responded to the request of the first responding officers who were called to the Ashley residence. The police investigators highlighted areas within the house, which were assumed to be the entry and exit points of the suspect, plus the master bedroom, which is the main homicide scene. The crime scene technicians processed the entire Ashley residence and recovered roughly 100 different latent impressions. The majority of the latent and patent prints found at the scene were identified to be those of William and Jane Ashley based on elimination fingerprints collected at the medical examiner's office during the autopsy. Eight impressions have yet to be identified, which means they could have been left by the suspect.

INTRODUCTION TO FINGERPRINTS

Processing at a crime scene involves three different types of fingerprint impressions: latent, patent, and plastic. A latent print is not visible to the naked eye, which means a person must process the scene and enhance the latent print using black powder or chemicals. A patent print is visible without processing and includes fingerprints left in blood, oil, and dirt. A plastic print is a three-dimensional impression where the friction ridge skin of the finger sinks into a surface, such as window caulk.

Types of Fingerprint Patterns

Once fingerprints have been located at a crime scene, either the item is collected or the print is powdered and lifted using tape or a fingerprint lifter. The recovered print is then identified as one of the three main categories of prints and then as one of the eight possible fingerprint pattern subcategories.

Three main categories of fingerprint patterns:
- loop
- arch
- whorl

Eight subcategories of fingerprint patterns:
- ulnar loop
- radial loop
- plain arch
- tented arch
- plain whorl
- central pocket loop whorl
- double loop whorl
- accidental whorl

Loop

A loop is a pattern in which the ridges of the print enter on one side, curve in the middle, and exit out the same side. The loop is the most common type of fingerprint pattern and can be subclassified as either an ulnar loop or a radial loop. An ulnar loop has the opening of the ridges pointing toward the little finger of the hand, which is closest to the ulna bone of the forearm. A radial loop has the opening of the ridges pointing toward the thumb of the hand, which is closest to the radial bone of the forearm.

Loop. iStockphoto.

Arch

An arch is a pattern in which the ridges enter on one side of the print and exit out the opposite side with a slight rise in the center. The arch can be subclassified as either a plain arch or a tented arch. A plain arch has a slight rise in the center of the print, as opposed to a tented arch, which has a very steep rise in the center of the print.

Arch. iStockphoto.

Whorl

A whorl is a pattern in which the ridges have a circular or swirled center. A whorl can be subclassified as a plain whorl, a central pocket loop whorl, a double loop whorl, or an accidental whorl.

Fingerprint Processing

In order to visualize latent prints at a crime scene, the crime scene technician must use fingerprint powder and a fingerprint brush to dust the areas where suspected fingerprints are located. When a darkened fingerprint is exposed with the brush-and-powder technique, the fingerprint can then be lifted as evidence and saved for future comparisons at the crime laboratory. All enhanced fingerprints at crime scenes should be saved even if you cannot determine the pattern type with the naked eye.

Whorl. iStockphoto.

Enhanced fingerprints can be lifted using tape, which can be specific crime scene fingerprint tape or clear packing tape. The tape should be large enough to cover the entire impression. If the impression is large, such as a palm, multiple pieces of tape can be used to create one lift. Place the tape on one edge of the impression and slowly cover the impression with the tape. Once the impression is covered completely, remove the tape from the surface and place it on a fingerprint backer. A fingerprint backer contains information regarding the crime scene on one side and a blank surface for the tape lift on the opposite side. Place the tape lift on the backer and complete the relevant crime scene information. Once the fingerprint lifter is filled out, the item can be cataloged and packaged as evidence.

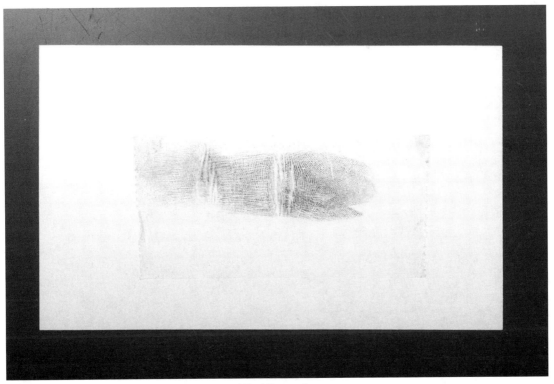

Lifted fingerprint.

Fingerprint backer.

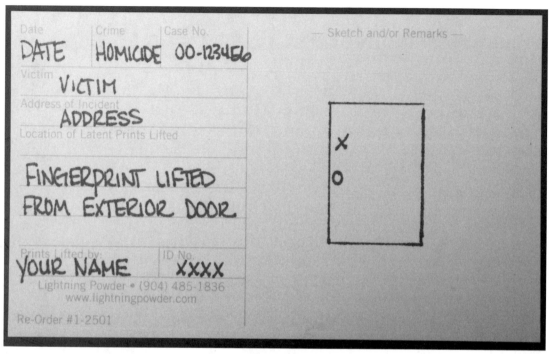

Filled-out fingerprint backer.

PRELAB ACTIVITY REVIEW AND PRACTICE

Define the Following Terms

arch
latent print
loop
patent print
plastic print
whorl

Practice Exercises

The crime scene technicians processed the entire Ashley residence and recovered roughly 100 different latent impressions. The majority of the latent and patent prints found at the scene were identified to be those of William and Jane Ashley. Eight impressions could not be identified to William or Jane Ashley, which means the remaining fingerprints could have been left by the suspect.

Using the fingerprint impressions listed earlier recovered from various places in the Ashley residence, label the different patterns (loop, arch, and whorl).

Fingerprint 1.

Fingerprint 2.

Fingerprint 3.

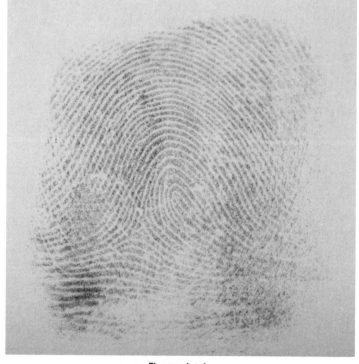

Fingerprint 4.

Fingerprint 5.

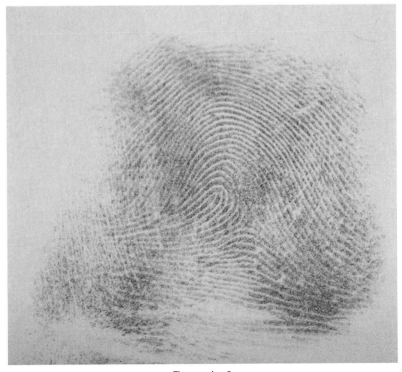

Fingerprint 6.

Fingerprint 7.

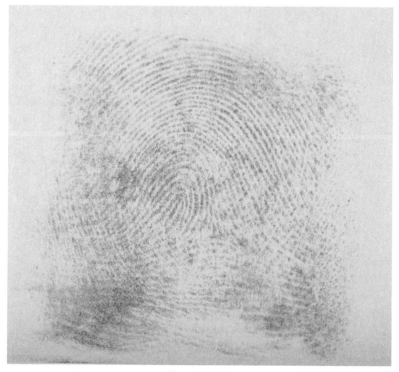

Fingerprint 8.

5.2

LABORATORY EXERCISE: FINGERPRINT PROCESSING

CLASSROOM AND ONLINE INSTRUCTIONS

Classroom Course—If you are completing Laboratory #5 in a classroom setting, you can place fingerprints on a soda or water bottle and see if you can visualize the patterns. Then look at your own hand and try to link the fingerprint on the can or bottle to one of your 10 fingerprints.

Online Course—If you are completing Laboratory #5 in an online course, you can place fingerprints on items around your house, such as a glass window. See if you can visualize the fingerprint and identify the pattern without the need for processing.

Materials List

- Soda can, plastic bottle, or glass bottle
- Black fingerprint powder (could substitute with copier toner)
- Feather brush or artistic paint brush
- Clear packing tape
- Blank index cards
- Pen or marker

The Exercise

1. Place fingerprint impressions on an empty clean soda can. If you have dry hands, you can rub your fingers behind your ear in order to apply grease to your hands to ensure leaving behind good fingerprints.
2. If you have access to black fingerprint powder, apply the powder to the soda can using a feather brush. If you do not

have a synthetic or feather fingerprint brush, you can always use a paint brush purchased at an art store.

3. Once you have powdered the soda can, see if you visualize any darkened fingerprint impressions. You can tilt the can to the light in order to visualize the prints better.

4. Using a piece of clear packing tape, place the tape directly over the powdered fingerprint impression on the can. To prevent air bubbles and creases in the tape, work from one side of the tape to the other side. Lift the tape off of the soda can and place it on a blank index card or piece of card stock.

5. Fill out the back of the blank index card or card stock with the relevant fingerprint lifting information.

6. Repeat steps 1–5 until you have completed and lifted five fingerprint impressions.

7. Using the incident report located in the appendix, complete one incident report explaining your methods for visualizing, enhancing, and lifting the fingerprints.

8. Using the evidence submission form located in the appendix, complete the evidence form and submit the five fingerprint lifts to the crime laboratory for comparison.

9. Using the chain of custody form located in the appendix, complete the chain of custody to track the evidence from the crime scene to court.

LABORATORY #6 FINGERPRINT 10-PRINT CARD

CHAPTER OUTLINE
6.1 Introduction to Fingerprint 10-Print Card
6.2 Laboratory Exercise: Fingerprint 10-Print Card

LEARNING OBJECTIVES

- Identify a 10-print fingerprint card
- Understand the completion of the three sections of the fingerprint card
- Explain the techniques used to roll fingers
- Demonstrate the proper completion of a fingerprint card

WHAT YOU WILL LEARN

Laboratory #6, Fingerprint 10-Print Card, introduces the student to various techniques for completion of an inked fingerprint card. The three sections of a traditional fingerprint card are explained with examples, and the techniques necessary to produce a high-quality card are included. The chapter ends with a laboratory exercise to show proficiency with completing an inked fingerprint card and completion of required paperwork.

KEY TERMS
identifying information
inked prints
plain impressions
rolled impressions
10-print card

CASE FILE 00-123456: FINGERPRINT 10-PRINT CARD

The crime scene technicians processed the entire Ashley residence and found multiple patent and latent fingerprints throughout the house. Most of the fingerprints were compared to elimination standards taken from both victims at the medical examiner's office. The remaining eight fingerprints found in the house need to be compared to potential witnesses and suspects. Since Lynette Saunders admitted to being in the residence to walk the dogs, the police requested elimination fingerprints to be taken from her. During the course of the investigation, the police identified three other individuals who recently had access to the Ashley residence and were needed to eliminate some of the unidentified prints found at the scene. The police requested elimination standards to be completed by John Lee, Doug Parsons, and Antonia Sanchez and then comparisons to the remaining eight fingerprints.

INTRODUCTION TO FINGERPRINT 10-PRINT CARD

Inked prints are patent or visible to the naked eye due to the fact that reproduction of the friction ridge skin is completed using black printers' ink. An inked fingerprint card is completed by law enforcement at the time of arrest, for employment applications, and for pistol permits. The fingerprint card or 10-print card is arranged into three sections: information, rolled impressions, and plain impressions. The information section on the card contains relevant data regarding the person being printed and the

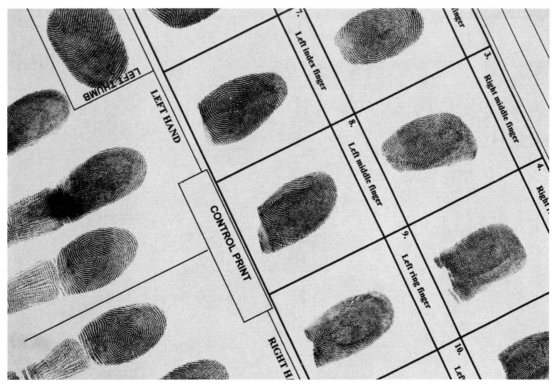

Sample FBI fingerprint card. iStockphoto.

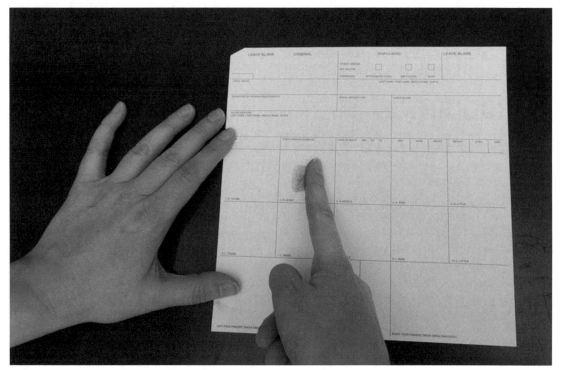

Fingerprinting.

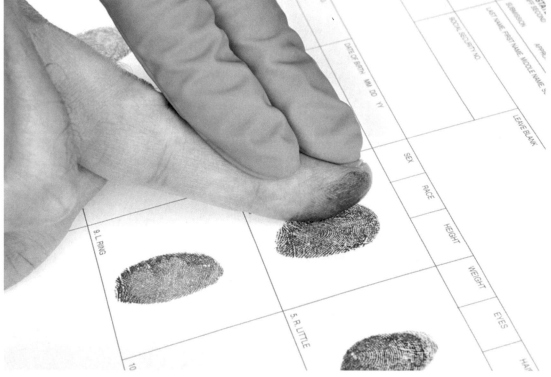

Investigator fingerprinting. iStockphoto.

individual completing the card. The rolled impression portion of the card contains 10 individual fingers rolled from nail to nail. The plain or flat impression portion of the card contains the 10 fingerprints placed directly onto the card.

A fingerprint card is arranged by right hand over left hand, always starting at the right thumb and moving through to the right little and then left thumb to left little.

When rolling a fingerprint, the investigator should have a firm hold of the hand or finger of the individual and start with finger #1, right thumb and work through to finger #10, left little. Each finger should be checked for proper ink distribution and rolled from one side to the other side. Never roll back and forth because this will cause a distortion of the ridge detail!

PRELAB ACTIVITY REVIEW AND PRACTICE

Define the Following Terms

identifying information
inked prints
plain impressions
rolled impressions
10-print card

Investigative Tip

Have the individual being fingerprinted remain loose in order to prevent smudging or distorting the inked fingerprint images.

Practice Exercises

The eight fingerprint impressions recovered by the crime scene technicians labeled in the previous lab have been identified.
- One fingerprint on the back door of the Ashley residence was identified as Doug Parsons
- Four fingerprints on the front staircase were identified as Antonia Sanchez
- One fingerprint on the front door was identified as Lynette Saunders
- One fingerprint on the master bedroom door was identified as Doug Parsons

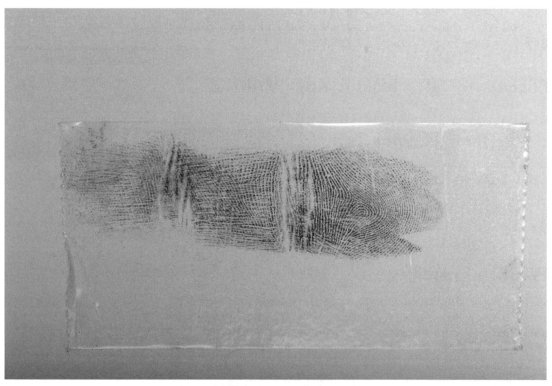

Fingerprint lift from master bedroom door.

6.2

LABORATORY EXERCISE: FINGERPRINT 10-PRINT CARD

CLASSROOM AND ONLINE INSTRUCTIONS

Classroom Course—If you are completing Laboratory #6 in a classroom setting, you can use specific fingerprint ink or a rubber stamper. Make copies of the blank fingerprint card and practice rolling each finger. As you are inking the finger and rolling, look at the darkened detail on your finger. Can you see any distortions, such as a scar?

Online Course—If you are completing Laboratory #6 in an online course, you can use a rubber stamper, preferably with blank ink, and a blank sheet of white paper to practice rolling fingerprint impressions. You can roll each finger and then attempt to ink your entire palm so you can visualize the ridge detail located on this friction ridge surface.

Materials List

- Fingerprint ink pad or black rubber stamper pad
- Pen
- A volunteer you can fingerprint

The Exercise

1. Select a person to fingerprint.
2. Using the blank fingerprint card located in the appendix, complete the information on the fingerprint card.
3. If you have access to a fingerprint pad you can use this, otherwise use a rubber stamping pad (preferably black ink) and complete the fingerprint card by rolling all 10 fingers and then the plain impressions at the bottom.
4. Using the blank incident report located in the appendix, complete a report detailing completion of the 10-print fingerprint card.

5. Using the blank evidence submission form in the appendix, complete the submission form so that the fingerprint card can be transferred to the forensic laboratory for comparison to fingerprints recovered from the scene.
6. Using the blank chain of custody form in the appendix, complete the chain of custody to document the transfer of the fingerprint card from the police station or scene to the forensic laboratory.

7

LABORATORY #7 QUESTIONED DOCUMENT EXAMINATION

CHAPTER OUTLINE

LEARNING OBJECTIVES

- Understand questioned document examination and the various analysis techniques
- Explain the difference between known writing and exemplars
- Identify the equipment used within the questioned document field
- Analyze handwriting samples for similarities and differences
- Complete exemplar samples

WHAT YOU WILL LEARN

Laboratory #7, Questioned Document Examination, introduces the student to various techniques used by the forensic document examiner (FDE) to analyze evidence. Each specific form of analysis is identified and explained to illustrate the techniques used to enhance writing. The two main pieces of equipment, the electrostatic detection device (EDD) and the video spectral comparator (VSC), are explained based on the type of document case presented to the forensic examiner. Handwriting analysis is explained with information on how to analyze a sample or collect an exemplar for comparison purposes. The chapter ends with a laboratory exercise to show proficiency with analyzing handwriting, collecting exemplars, and packaging document evidence with the completion of required paperwork.

KEY TERMS

alteration
forged writing
handwriting comparison
indented writing

known writing
obliteration
questioned writing

CASE FILE 00-123456: DOCUMENT EXAMINATION

The crime scene technicians processed the entire Ashley residence and located multiple items that could be considered evidence. One potential piece of evidence recovered from the scene was a blank pad of paper. The blank pad of paper was processed by the document examiner using the EDD. A series of numbers were enhanced after processing with the EDD, and the numbers corresponded to the bank accounts of both William and Jane Ashley.

The numbers were:

7008346578

7008559762

Antonia Sanchez, Jane Ashley's personal assistant, also provided the police with a death threat sent to the family 2 weeks prior to the homicide. The letter was processed for fingerprints, but with no results. The document examiner requested handwriting samples for the three possible suspects (Doug Parsons, John Lee, and Antonia Sanchez) so a comparison could be made between the known samples and the handwriting from the death threat note.

INTRODUCTION TO DOCUMENT EXAMINATION

Introduction

Document examination encompasses a wide range of topics involving the writing source, writing medium, and type of paper. A forensic document examiner could be responsible for analyzing handwriting samples to determine forgeries, indented writing on paper, obliterations or alterations of existing writing, paper and ink sources, and authenticity of documents. At a crime scene, items collected for document examination must be collected and packaged carefully so as not to destroy the sample or inadvertently write on the packaging and alter the sample.

Investigation Sequence

Document examination is always completed first in the crime laboratory evidence processing sequence as methods used by other disciplines, such as latent print analysis, can destroy the writing sample and ink on the paper. First, the document evidence is photographed or copied in order to retain an accurate, original representation of the sample prior to testing and comparison. Next, the document examiner can use different wavelengths of light to enhance or visualize the ink samples better. Depending on the type of examination, light sources, magnification, and machines can be used to assist in the comparison process.

Handwriting Examination

Handwriting examination is one of the principal tasks performed by forensic document examiners. Handwriting examinations are conducted by analyzing, comparing, and evaluating questioned documents or the item of evidence versus known writings or samples that can be linked to the suspect, such as handwriting in a personal notebook. The FDE utilizes

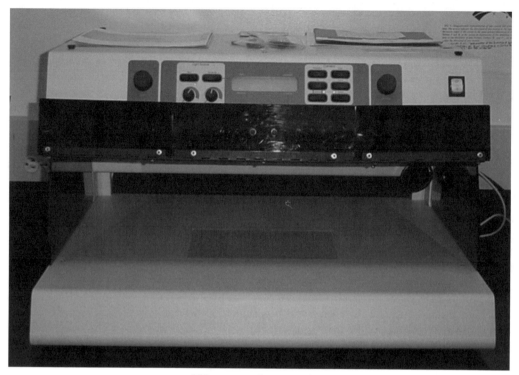

Video spectral comparator.

a stereomicroscope, along with hand magnifiers, to assist in conducting a detailed examination of the evidence. Upon completion of the examination process, the FDE will express an opinion that can range from identification to elimination of a writer. This range also includes qualified opinions, which are in between identification and elimination.

When a person writes on paper, the surface of the paper is altered or compressed by the writing instrument, which creates an indentation on both the original layer of paper and the next few layers of paper. The indentations, which may be visible to the naked eye, are typically enhanced using oblique or side lighting and a piece of equipment known as an electrostatic detection device (EDD). An EDD is an instrument used by the document examiner to enhance indented writing on a document in a safe, nondestructive manner. First, a thin sheet of Mylar is placed over the sample in question to protect the original document from destruction. Then an electrostatic charge is applied to the evidence. Black toner

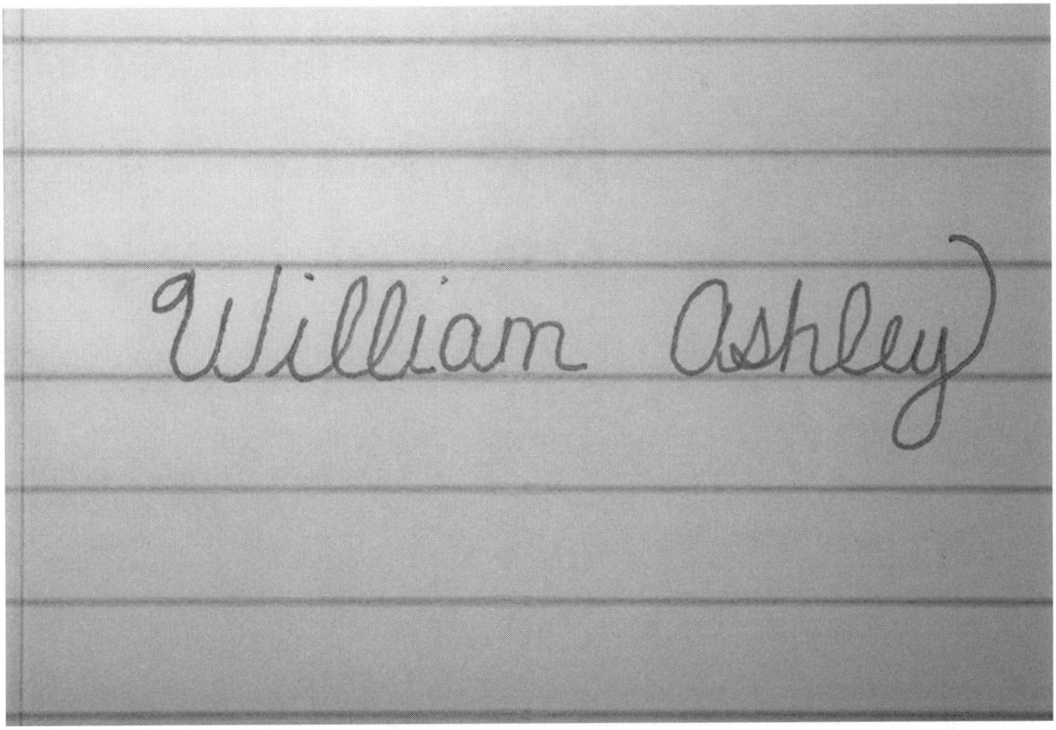
William Ashley

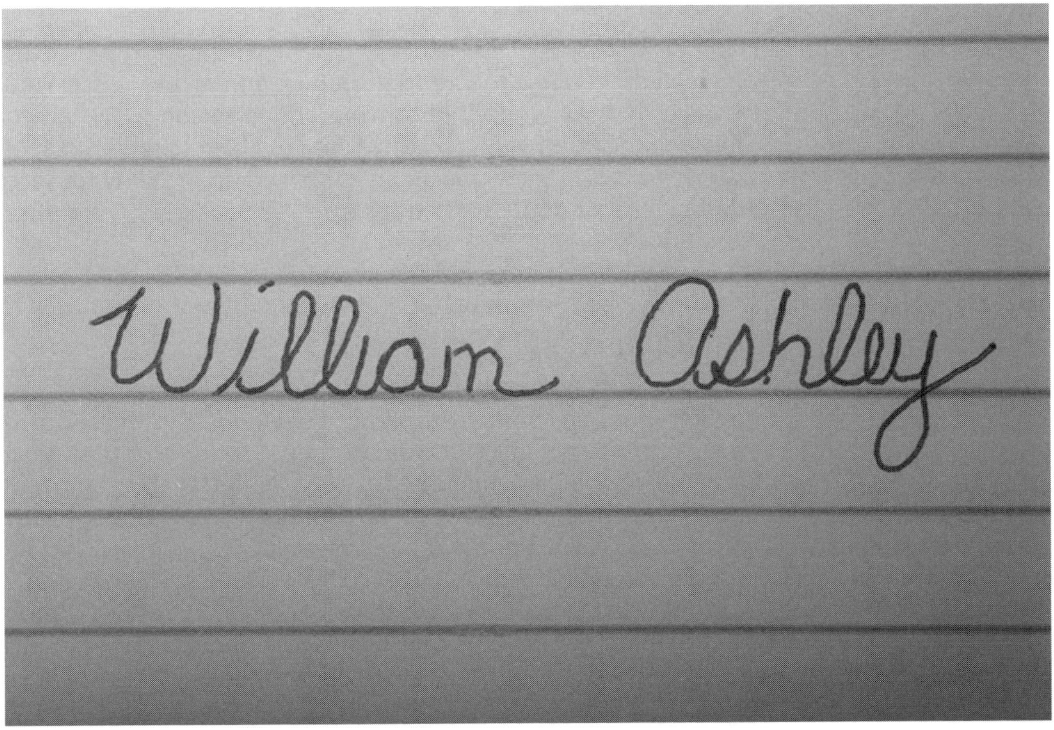
William Ashley

Handwriting samples.

powder is applied to the Mylar sheet under the electrostatic charge and any indented writing clings to the black powder for enhancement. Finally, the Mylar sheet is removed and preserved as a new piece of evidence or lifted in order to depict the indented writing from the original sample of evidence.

Alterations and Obliterations

A document examiner also examines cases of alterations and obliterations in order to separate the original source from the modification. An alteration is an adjustment or change to the original text of the document. Obliteration is the removal of material contained within the original document through either an erasure or a deliberate action to obstruct the writing. The video spectral comparator (VSC) is a tool used by document examiners to apply various wavelengths of light and filters to analyze altered and obliterated text on a questioned document.

Investigative Tip

You may remember as a child that you could reveal indented writing by shading the surface with the side of a pencil, causing the indented writing to darken. Never use shading as a forensic technique, as darkening of the indented writing obstructs the use of other forensic techniques and can ruin the evidence.

Electrostatic detection device.

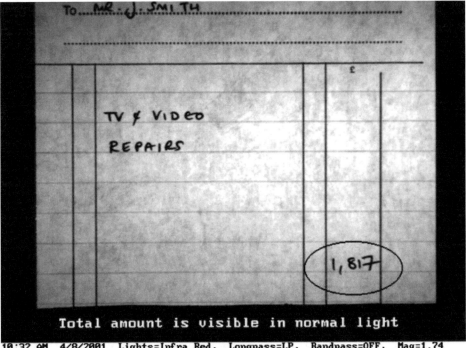

Altered receipt.

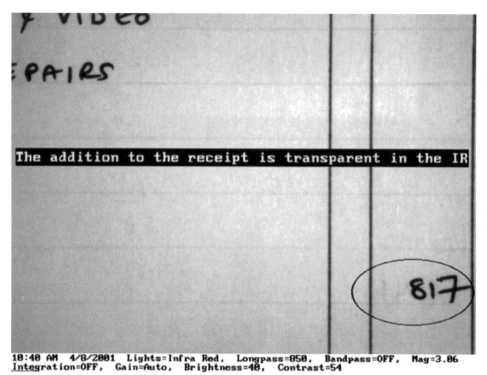

The addition to the receipt is transparent in the IR

10:40 AM 4/8/2001 Lights=Infra Red, Longpass=850, Bandpass=OFF, Mag=3.06
Integration=OFF, Gain=Auto, Brightness=40, Contrast=54

Close-up of altered receipt.

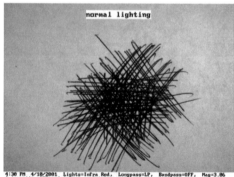

normal lighting

4:30 PM 4/10/2001 Lights=Infra Red, Longpass=LP, Bandpass=OFF, Mag=3.86
Integration=OFF, Gain=Auto, Brightness=40, Contrast=54

4:31 PM 4/10/2001 Lights=Infra Red, Longpass=735, Bandpass=OFF, Mag=3.06
Integration=OFF, Gain=Auto, Brightness=48, Contrast=54

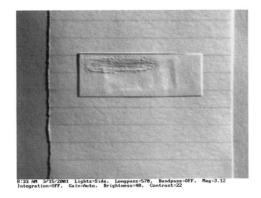

8:33 AM 3/15/2001 Lights=Side, Longpass=570, Bandpass=OFF, Mag=3.12
Integration=OFF, Gain=Auto, Brightness=48, Contrast=22

8:34 AM 3/15/2001 Lights=Transmitted, Longpass=570, Bandpass=OFF, Mag=3.12
Integration=OFF, Gain=Auto, Brightness=48, Contrast=54

Obliterations.

PRELAB ACTIVITY REVIEW AND PRACTICE

Define the Following Terms

alteration
forged writing
handwriting comparison
indented writing
known writing
obliteration
questioned writing

Practice Exercises

A death threat note was provided to the police by Antonia Sanchez, Jane Ashley's personal assistant. The document examiner analyzed the note and requested handwriting samples from Doug Parsons, John Lee, and Antonia Sanchez.

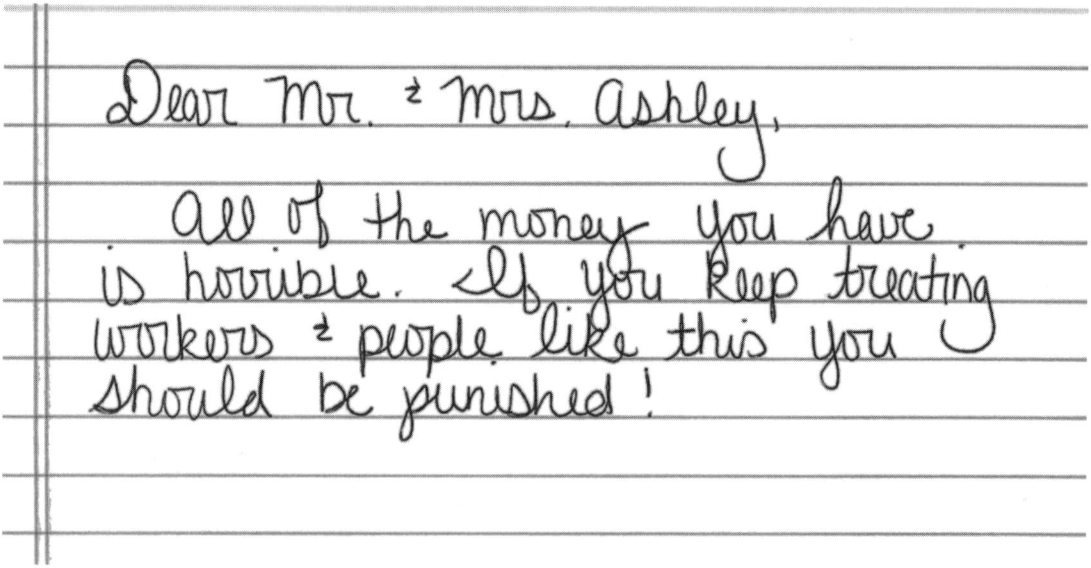

Death threat note.

Compare the handwriting in the death threat note to the three samples from Doug Parsons, John Lee, and Antonia Sanchez. Identify any similar characteristics between the evidence and the known samples.

I am writing this exemplar
for the police and the forensic
document examiner.

Signature sample of Doug Parsons.

I AM WRITING THIS EXEMPLAR FOR
THE POLICE AND THE FORENSIC DOCUMENT

EXAMINER.

Signature sample of John Lee.

al am writing this exemplar
for the police and the forensic
document examiner.

Signature sample of Antonia Sanchez.

LABORATORY EXERCISE: QUESTIONED DOCUMENT EXAMINATION

CLASSROOM AND ONLINE INSTRUCTIONS

Classroom Course—If you are completing Laboratory #7 in a classroom setting, use an item from the course, such as the syllabus, to shred for the laboratory exercise. Look in your notebook and see if your handwriting has changed throughout the class.

Online Course—If you are completing Laboratory #7 in an online course, look through your notebook to see if your writing has changed from the beginning of the semester until this point. See if you can find five items with your signature on them and then try to forge them.

Materials List

- Blank paper
- Assorted pens and markers
- Lined notebook paper
- Printed paper (you can use anything with text or pictures already printed)
- Clear tape

The Exercise

1. Take a sheet of blank paper and attempt to copy the signature listed below. If possible, try to use different writing utensils, such as a blue or black pen, a black marker, and a gel pen.
2. Take a sheet of lined paper and write the boldfaced phrase below 40 times in cursive. What do you notice about your handwriting from the first line of the phrase to the last line of the phrase?

   If you want to see your dog again bring $10,000 to the local dog park by noon!

3. Take two pieces of paper with text already printed on them and, using either a single shredder or a pair of scissors, cut the paper into small strips. Mix the strips together and attempt to reassemble the two pieces of paper. You can use clear tape to help hold the strips together.

4. Using a blank incident report located in the appendix, complete the incident report to document what you accomplished with handwriting comparisons and fracture matches.

LABORATORY #8 FOOTWEAR AND TIRE IMPRESSIONS

CHAPTER OUTLINE

8.1 Footwear and Tire Impressions

8.2 Laboratory Exercise: Footwear and Tire Impressions

LEARNING OBJECTIVES

- Understand the difference between class and individual characteristics
- Explain two- and three-dimensional impressions
- Demonstrate proper photography techniques for footwear and tire impression evidence
- Use techniques to collect both crime scene samples and known samples from evidence
- Comprehend the required crime scene paperwork

WHAT YOU WILL LEARN

Laboratory #8, Footwear and Tire Impressions, introduces the student to various techniques for identifying footwear and tire impressions at crime scenes. The techniques used to photograph and enhance evidence on both two- and three-dimensional surfaces are explained. Information on collection is included with examples of ways to complete dental stone casts, inked impressions, and Biofoam samples. Class and individual characteristics are used to explain the necessary requirements needed for a comparison within the forensic laboratory. The chapter ends with a laboratory exercise to show proficiency with locating footwear and tire impressions, as well as documenting the evidence through photography and completion of required paperwork.

KEY TERMS

class characteristics

individual characteristics

Criminalistics Laboratory Manual.

known shoes
tread
wear patterns

CASE FILE 00-123456: FOOTWEAR AND TIRE IMPRESSIONS

The crime scene technicians who responded to the Ashley double homicide processed the crime scene for potential evidence leading to the suspect. Because the victims were found deceased in the master bedroom and the police investigators determined the crime actually occurred in the master bedroom, the entire house was processed for evidence. The suspect must have entered the residence from the exterior side of the house and gained access through either a window or a door. The investigators determined that the basement windows were locked and did not exhibit any evidence that the dust around the sills had been disturbed recently. The crime scene investigators searched both the front and the rear entrance of the residence and found footwear impressions in dirt at the rear entrance to the house. There was also a visible footwear impression in the upstairs hallway that was presumed to be left in blood from the suspect.

FOOTWEAR AND TIRE IMPRESSIONS

Footwear Impressions

Footwear impression evidence found at a crime scene is considered either two or three dimensional depending on the surface where the impression was deposited. A two-dimensional surface, such as tile or wood floors, will allow a transfer of the flat sole of an item of footwear, whereas a three-dimensional surface, such as dirt or snow, will allow a transfer of not only the sole but also the depth of the tread and the sides of the shoe source.

When a potential crime has occurred, it is imperative that the first responder attempt to protect footwear evidence from damage or destruction during processing of the crime scene. Once a crime is reported, the scene may be entered by paramedics, investigators, crime scene technicians, the district attorney, and the medical examiner. This means there is a potential for additional footwear impressions to be left at the scene and footwear impressions left from the suspect to be destroyed.

Investigative Tip

Always remember to photograph the scene and evidence prior to lifting or casting footwear and tire impressions.

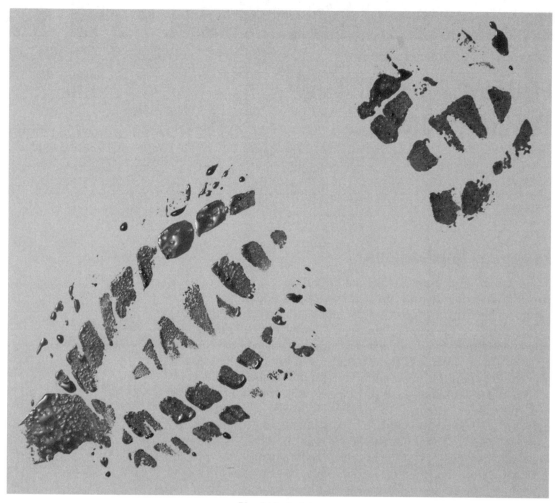

Bloody footprint.

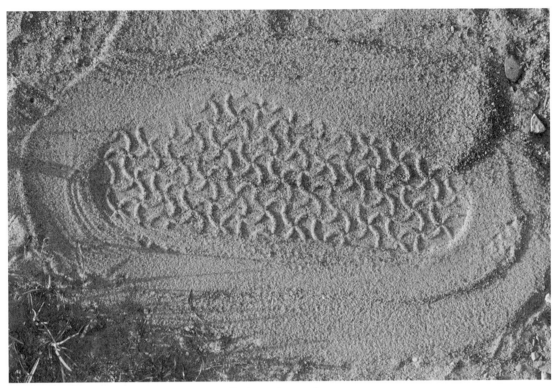

Footwear impression.

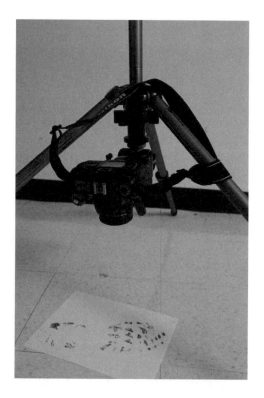

Photographing footwear evidence.

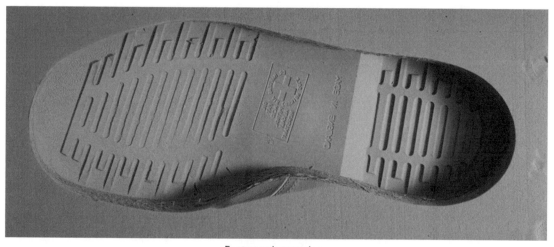

Footwear impression.

The first thing to do at a scene is to identify the potential impressions. One of the easiest ways to visualize latent or patent impressions is to use a flashlight and side light. This method works best for two-dimensional impressions deposited in dust or dirt on a hard surface, such as a tile floor. If three-dimensional impressions are visible in snow, mud, or sand, the tread pattern can be secured with dental stone casting. For individuals present at the scene, such as the investigators and medical examiner, a nondestructive method of capturing the footwear tread pattern can be made using inkless footwear impression kits and Biofoam casting boxes.

Prior to any casting or lifting of impression evidence, photography must be completed to document the scene. In some instances, the direction of impressions, the amount of footwear samples, and the space between each step need to be recorded for future scene recreations. The camera should be placed on top of a tripod and placed parallel to the surface of the impression. In order to make a comparison later on in your case, the footwear impression photographed at the scene must be

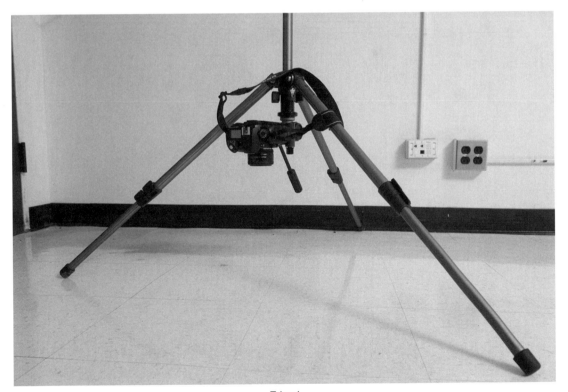

Tripod.

capable of being sized one-to-one. If the camera is not placed parallel to the surface of the impression, size cannot be generated at a later date, which means the photograph cannot be used for identification. A scale must also be included within each frame in order to denote the size of the overall impression.

Impression evidence can be compared and identified to a source using class characteristics and individual characteristics. Class characteristics are unique to a large group of items generated from the same manufacturer or source. An example of a class characteristic for footwear samples would be the manufacturer, such as Nike. The footwear impression at the scene could be narrowed down by class characteristics to a Nike Air Force One sneaker but could not be identified to a specific Nike Air Force One sneaker. Individual characteristics are unique to a single source. An example of individual characteristics for footwear samples would be cuts and gouges on the sole of the shoe, which could be linked back to a specific shoe.

Photographing footwear evidence.

Tire Impressions

Tire impressions are located, photographed, and lifted in the same manner as footwear evidence. The main difference between footwear impressions and tire impressions is the size of the continuous impression. In footwear cases, each sample is the size of one shoe, but in a tire case, the impression could be deposited in the mud for 20 feet. In order to photograph a continuous tire impression, each image can be taken with an overlap of the scale. This will allow the crime scene technician to print multiple photographs and place each picture together to recreate the entire impression at the scene.

Class and individual characteristics are also used in tire impression cases. An example of a class characteristic for tire impressions would be the tread design, which could correspond to a Goodyear brand tire. An example of individual characteristics for tire impressions would be cuts, gouges, or a nail imbedded in the tread.

Footprint. iStockphoto.

Tire impressions from vehicles parked at the crime scene from medical personnel, investigators, and technicians can obscure impressions left from the suspect and add additional impressions for comparison. In order to capture elimination standards of known vehicles, each of the four tires can be inked and rolled on long sheets of white butcher paper. A thin layer of petroleum jelly can also be applied to each of the four tires and rolled on butcher paper. Once the tires are rolled with petroleum jelly, a small amount of black powder can be applied to the clear impression.

PRELAB ACTIVITY REVIEW AND PRACTICE

Define the Following Terms

class characteristics
individual characteristics
known shoes
tread
wear patterns

Tire impression.

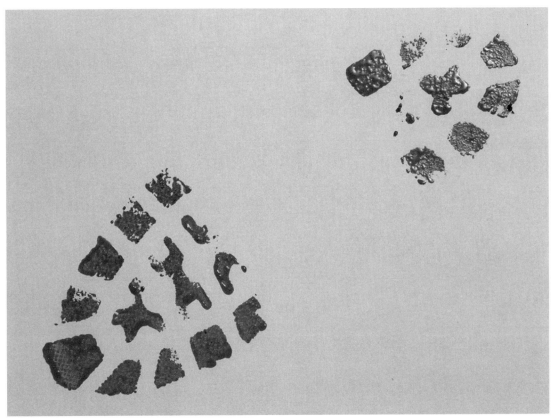

Crime scene impression.

Image A—Footwear recovered from Antonia Sanchez.

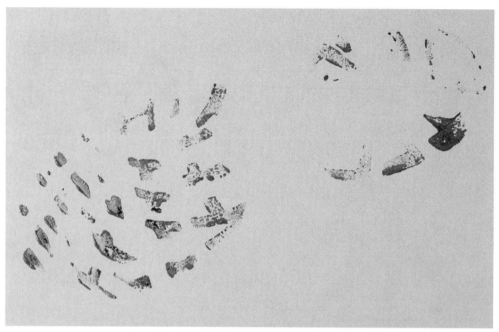

Image B—Footwear recovered from Officer Brown.

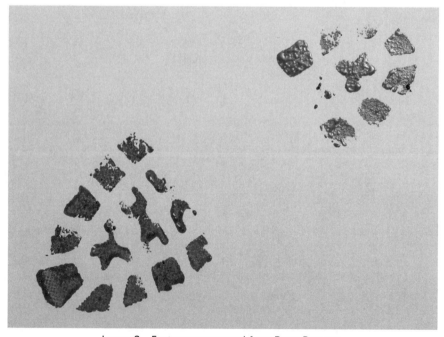

Image C—Footwear recovered from Doug Parsons.

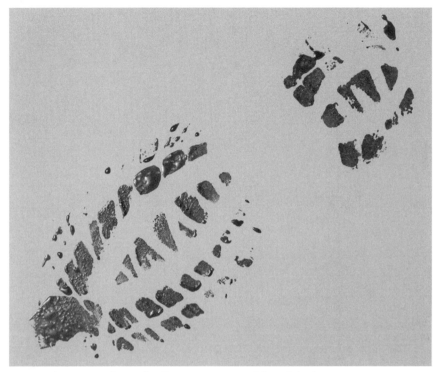

Image D—Footwear recovered from John Lee.

Practice Exercises

Using the picture of the footwear impression from the top of page 117, describe the class characteristics from the crime scene impression located outside the rear door of the Ashley residence. You should try to answer the following questions regarding the class characteristics:

- Is the tread visible?
- Is the tread pattern consistent with a work boot, sneaker, high heel, or dress shoe?
- What is the general pattern of the tread?
- Are there any identifying details that would tell you the brand of the footwear?

Circle any individual characteristics that could be used for comparison purposes.

Compare the class and individual characteristics from the crime scene footwear impression to the four possible shoes recovered from people involved in the case. Do any of the shoes listed here match the impression recovered at the crime scene?

LABORATORY EXERCISE: FOOTWEAR AND TIRE IMPRESSIONS

CLASSROOM AND ONLINE INSTRUCTIONS

Classroom Course—If you are completing Laboratory #8 in a classroom setting, use your current shoe and examine the sole for class and individual characteristics. Turn off the lights in the classroom and, using side lighting from a flashlight, illuminate the floor. See if you can find two-dimensional impressions on either the tile floor or the carpet.

Online Course—If you are completing Laboratory #8 in an online course, use a pair of shoes that have been worn and examine the soles for class and individual characteristics. If you want to view the tread in a crime scene setting, wear the shoes and walk through dirt, leaving a three-dimensional impression. You can then walk across a plain white sheet of paper to transfer the dirt pattern.

Materials

- One pair of shoes
- Outside area with loose dirt or sand
- Digital camera (minimum eight megapixels)
- Tripod
- Ruler or scale
- Blank paper
- Black fingerprint ink (can substitute with black shoe polish)
- Pen

Exercise

1. Take one set of shoes and examine the tread on the bottom of the shoes, assuming these are the known impressions from your suspect. Describe the detail in the tread and include

any class and individual characteristics present. Also, describe any information from the shoe, such as make, model, and size.

2. Find some loose dirt or sand outside of the classroom and, while wearing the shoes, place an impression in the dirt or sand, making a crime scene impression.

3. Photograph the footwear impression using a scale to depict the size.

4. Compare the photograph of the impression to the actual tread on the shoe and see if any individual characteristics were reproduced in the crime scene impression. List the characteristics that you can see between the crime scene impression and the actual shoes.

5. Take one sheet of computer paper, one pair of shoes, and black fingerprint ink. Carefully ink the bottom of the shoes with the black fingerprint ink and apply pressure to the shoes on the computer paper.

6. Examine the inked footwear impression to see if any class and individual characteristics were reproduced on the crime scene print.

7. Using the incident report located in the appendix, complete an incident report describing your methods for comparison and the results of the comparison.

Investigative Tip

Crime scene technicians will take photographs of footwear impressions and will also cast the footwear impressions using dental stone.

LABORATORY #9 TOOL MARKS

CHAPTER OUTLINE

9.1 Tool Mark Impressions
9.2 Laboratory Exercise: Tool Marks

LEARNING OBJECTIVES

- Identify the markings associated with tool mark impressions
- Explain the three types of impression markings
- Understand the photography techniques used for capturing detail regarding the impressions
- Explain the steps needed to cast and compare the tool mark impressions
- Comprehend the required crime scene paperwork

WHAT YOU WILL LEARN

Laboratory #9, Tool Marks, introduces the student to the three types of impression markings used by a forensic examiner to compare samples from crime scenes. Different impressions caused by various tools are examined to understand the techniques necessary for comparison. Collection with casting material is explained to illustrate the class and individual characteristics of the item. The chapter ends with a laboratory exercise to show proficiency with using casting material and completion of required paperwork.

KEY TERMS

casting material
class characteristics
compression marks
cutting marks
individual characteristics
sliding marks
striations

Case File 00-123456: Tool Mark Impressions

The rear entrance of the Ashley residence was found opened with visible tool mark impressions on both the door frame and the door. Crime scene technicians photographed the marks using close-up images and a scale. The crime scene technicians then casted the impressions using Mikrosil, which is a rubber like substance that can be molded to capture the detail in an impression.

During the search of the residence, a crowbar was found in the master bedroom next to the body of Mrs. Ashley. Based on the autopsy report, it was determined that the wounds from Mrs. Ashley's head matched the size, shape, and striations on the crowbar. The forensic tool mark examiner compared the crowbar to the impressions found on the rear exterior door of the residence to determine if the same weapon made the marks.

TOOL MARK IMPRESSIONS

Introduction

Tool mark impression evidence is typically found at scenes where either a door or a window has been pried open to gain entry to the property. Most tools, such as hammers, pry bars, and screwdrivers, have class and individual characteristics on the metal portion or tip of the item. The individual characteristics on tools are typically small scrapes and gouges in the metal, which, when placed in contact with another surface, will transfer in the impression. In some cases, the tool will be dyed or painted a color, such as a blue crowbar, and the paint or dye can also transfer to another surface, leaving not only a tool mark impression but also a paint transfer that can be used for comparison purposes.

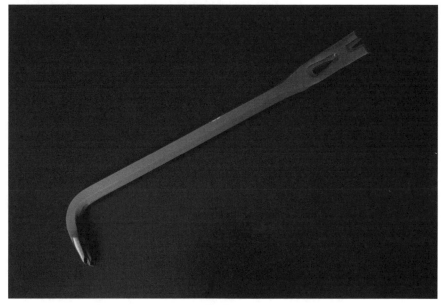

Pry bar.

Investigation

First, the tool mark impression must be photographed with a scale to show the size and location of each individual impression. Sometimes tool mark impressions on a surface, such as a wood window frame, can be linked back to the homeowner, while other impressions on the same window can be attributed to the individual entering the residence illegally. Once the tool mark impression has been photographed, a casting can be made. If the item can be removed from the scene, such as taking a door off of the hinges, it can be collected as evidence and processed at the crime laboratory. If the item cannot be removed from the scene, a casting using a compound known as putty can be made for future comparisons. Mikrosil is a common putty compound on the market that can be mixed at the scene.

Investigative Tip

Make sure you mix the Mikrosil when you are ready to cast because the casting putty hardens very quickly!

Mixing casting compound.

Once the putty cast has been made, there are two options for comparison. The first option is to also cast the item of evidence and compare the two putty casts together, looking for similar class and individual characteristics. The second option is to create a putty cast and then use the same dental stone material used for a footwear impression cast. The hard dental stone cast can then be compared to the actual piece of evidence, looking for similar class and individual characteristics.

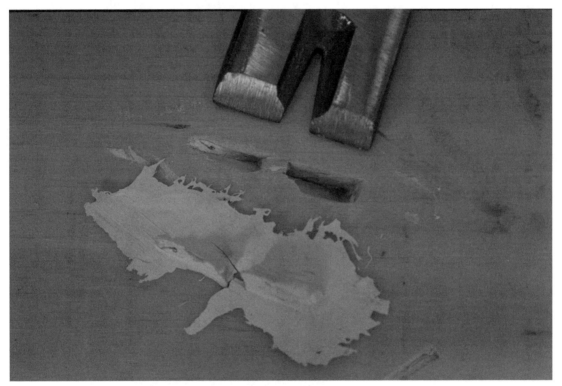

Taking a casting of tool marks.

PRELAB ACTIVITY REVIEW AND PRACTICE
Define the Following Terms

casting material
class characteristics
compression marks
cutting marks

individual characteristics
sliding marks
striations

Practice Exercises

Crime scene technicians cast the tool mark impressions found at the scene and collected the crowbar as evidence. The crowbar was submitted for fingerprints, and the latent print examiner reported an identification to Doug Parson, the plumber for the Ashley's. The crowbar and fingerprints could be explained easily as a tool of the plumbing trade, as Doug Parsons was recently completing a renovation job at the Ashley residence. However, if the crowbar marks are compared and identified to the tool marks found at the scene, Doug Parsons could be considered a suspect.

Use the photographs of the tool mark impressions below and compare them to the images of the tools to determine if any match.

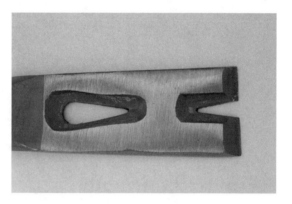

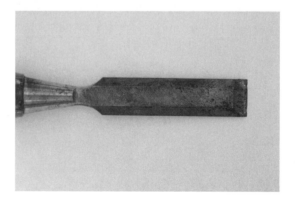

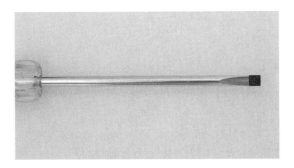

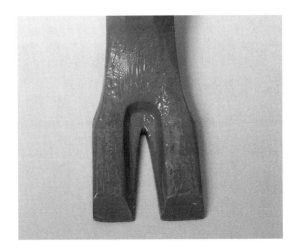

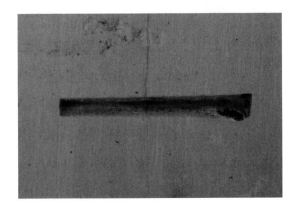

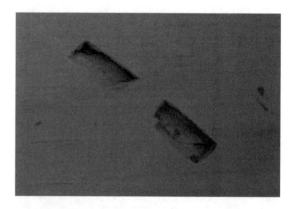

LABORATORY EXERCISE: TOOL MARKS

CLASSROOM AND ONLINE INSTRUCTIONS

Classroom Course—If you are completing Laboratory #9 in a classroom setting, place the tip of a screwdriver under a microscope and examine the characteristics of the metal. Observe the tip and, if possible, compare the image to other screwdrivers to see if there are individual characteristics present.

Online Course—If you are completing Laboratory #9 in an online course, see if you have multiple screwdrivers at home. Examine the tip of each screwdriver to see if there are different characteristics, such as the size and shape, plus individual scratches or gouges.

Materials List

- Piece of lumber
- Assortment of tools (screwdriver, crowbar, or hammer)
- Digital camera (minimum eight megapixels)
- Flashlight
- Modeling clay or putty
- Pen

The Exercise

1. Take a small piece of lumber and, using various types of tools, such as a crowbar, screwdriver, and hammer, leave small tool mark impressions in the wood.
2. Try to photograph the impressions and use some of the lighting techniques, such as side lighting with a flashlight, to visualize the unique characteristics identified with each tool.
3. Using modeling clay or putty, cast the impressions for comparison.

4. Identify class and individual characteristics found in the impression of the modeling clay or putty and the tool used to leave the impression.
5. Using the blank incident report located in the appendix, complete one incident report to describe the comparison and list the identifying characteristics.

LABORATORY #10 ODONTOLOGY

CHAPTER OUTLINE

10.1 Odontology
10.2 Laboratory Exercise: Odontology

LEARNING OBJECTIVES

- Understand the physical characteristics of the mandible and maxilla
- Identify bite mark impressions
- Explain the characteristics of bite mark impressions
- Compare samples of bite marks
- Understand the different methods used to capture a bite mark impression
- Comprehend the required crime scene paperwork

WHAT YOU WILL LEARN

Laboratory #10, Odontology, introduces the student to the discipline of forensic dentistry to understand the techniques used to identify a bite mark impression. The use of forensic odontology is explained to illustrate when the discipline can be used to assist with an identification. The characteristics of bite mark impressions, the human tooth structure, and primary and secondary dentition are explained. The methods used to capture and enhance bite mark evidence for comparisons are addressed to explain the different techniques that can be used based on the circumstances of the case. The chapter ends with a laboratory exercise to show proficiency with capturing and enhancing bite mark impression evidence and completion of required paperwork.

KEY TERMS

bite mark impression
mandible
maxilla
odontology
primary dentition
secondary dentition

CASE FILE 00-123456: ODONTOLOGY

The crime scene technicians and the medical examiner who responded to the Ashley double homicide noticed a bite mark on the right arm of William Ashley. The bite mark was photographed with a scale for a comparison to the possible suspects.

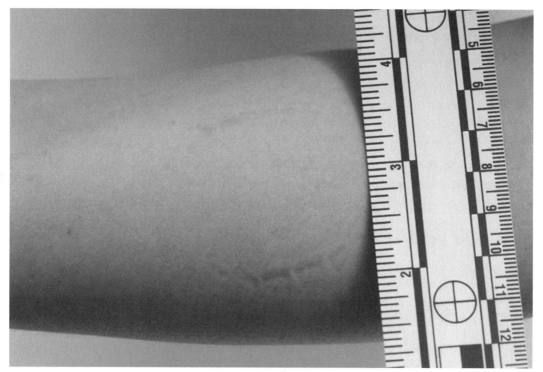

Bite mark.

When the police interviewed the potential suspects (Doug Parsons, John Lee, and Antonia Sanchez), it was noted that Antonia Sanchez had a mark on her right leg that she explained as a bite mark from Gracie the Chihuahua obtained while working at the Ashley residence. Antonia Sanchez said Gracie was always vicious and nipped at her ankles frequently. Doug Parsons also had a wound on his left leg, which could also be a bite mark. Doug Parsons did not have a specific explanation for the wound and said he probably cut himself on a pipe while he was working a plumbing job.

ODONTOLOGY

Introduction

Forensic odontology or forensic dentistry is the analysis of bite mark impressions or dental impressions in order to make an identification. During the course of a person's life, there are two forms of dentition: primary and permanent. Primary dentition forms around the 1-year mark and continues through childhood until the teeth, sometimes referred to as baby teeth, fall out. Permanent dentition forms after the primary tooth has been extracted and remains with the individual for the remainder of life. When a forensic odontologist analyzes the tooth structure or bite mark for identification purposes, the two structures of the

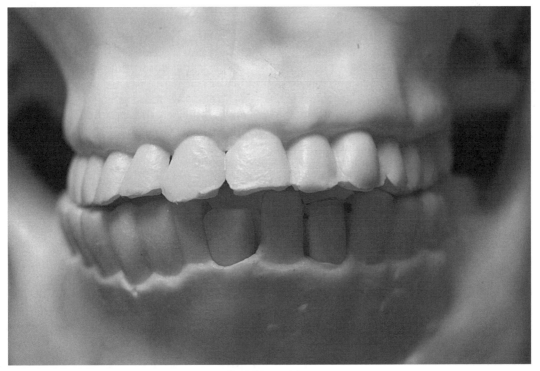

Dental impression.

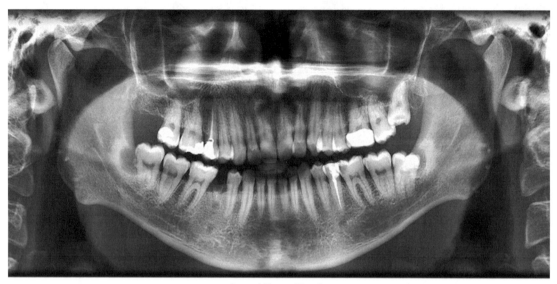

Dental X-ray. iStock.

jaw must be distinguished. The maxilla, or upper jaw, has different categories of teeth and structure compared with the mandible, the lower jaw. In some instances, the upper or lower jaw may be more prominent in the dental impression left at a scene. Forensic odontology can be used for the identification of a victim or individual where visual confirmation cannot be used due to decomposition of the body. In the case of victim identification, the forensic odontologist obtains an X-ray of the teeth attached to the skull and compares the information to known X-rays from suspected individuals. Once the X-rays are compared for consistencies, such as structure and shape of the tooth, filling location, and/or unique dental structures, a decision on identification can be made.

Investigation

Bite mark comparison and identification is another form of odontology used by a forensic dentist to analyze samples from a victim or item and link them back to a source, such as an individual's dentition. In order to analyze a bite mark impression, it must be photographed with a scale to show the accurate size of the wound and tooth structure. In some instances, the bite mark impression may not be as visible and defined on the first day, which means an investigator and crime scene technician should take multiple photographs over the course of 5 to 7 days. Once the bite mark impression and the surrounding skin start to heal and a bruise forms, the teeth indentations in the skin can be more pronounced and visible for comparison purposes.

PRELAB ACTIVITY REVIEW AND PRACTICE

Define the Following Terms

bite mark impression
mandible
maxilla
primary dentition
secondary dentition

Practice Exercises

Police investigators discovered two potential bite marks located on the lower legs of Antonia Sanchez and Doug Parsons. Since Gracie the Chihuahua is currently missing from the Ashley

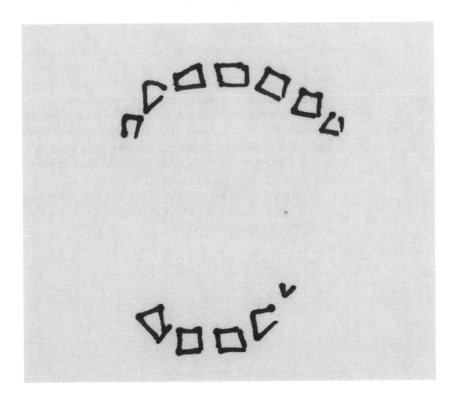

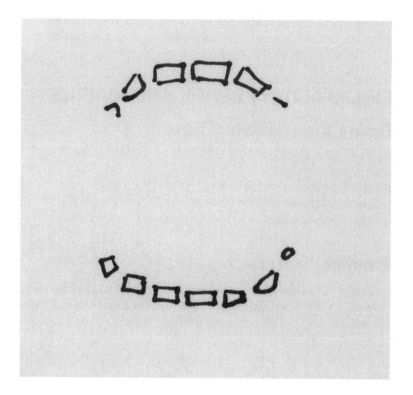

residence, an elimination cast of her teeth could not be obtained by the forensic odontologist. The forensic odontologist could compare the two samples from the potential suspects. Antonia Sanchez has already admitted that the bite mark on her leg was attributed to Gracie nipping at her ankles, which means a tentative comparison can be made.

Compare the tracings from the two bite marks and label any similarities between the two impressions. Do you think they were made by the same source?

LABORATORY EXERCISE: ODONTOLOGY

CLASSROOM AND ONLINE INSTRUCTIONS

Classroom Course—If you are completing Laboratory #10 in a classroom setting, you can use an anatomical skeleton from a science classroom to observe the maxilla and mandible. You can also lightly bite the edge of a Styrofoam cup to observe your bite mark impression.

Online Course—If you are completing Laboratory #10 in an online course, you can inquire with your dentist to see your past dental X-rays. Observe the X-rays to see if anything has changed over time, such as new fillings.

Materials

- Transparency paper, overlay paper, or clear sheet protector
- Black permanent marker
- Modeling clay or putty
- Pen

The Exercise

1. Using your nonwriting arm, gently bite down for 20–30 seconds on an area with little to no hair.
2. After 20–30 seconds of biting you should be able to visualize small teeth impressions in your arm. Look at the impressions and identify the upper and lower jaw; note any gaps between the teeth or shifted teeth.
3. Using a piece of clear overlay paper (this can be clear acetate or clear overlay paper for copiers) and a permanent marker, trace the outline of each tooth impression. This will help you visualize the size, shape, and spacing between each tooth.
4. Using modeling clay or putty, place a small, thin amount over the bite mark on your arm to capture the detail of the impression.

5. Place the clear piece of overlay paper over the putty cast of the impression and see if you can align the similarities.
6. Using the blank incident report located in the appendix, complete one report documenting the steps taken to compare the bite mark impression.

LABORATORY #11 BLOOD TYPING AND BIOLOGICAL FLUIDS

CHAPTER OUTLINE

11.1 Blood Typing and Biological Fluids
11.2 Laboratory Exercise: Biological Fluids

LEARNING OBJECTIVES

- Identify the four blood types
- Understand the differences among biological fluids
- Explain the use of blood typing in a forensic setting
- Understand the collection of biological fluids at a crime scene
- Comprehend the required crime scene paperwork

WHAT YOU WILL LEARN

Laboratory #11, Blood Typing and Biological Fluids, introduces the student to alternative evidence found at crime scenes that can assist with DNA identification. The four blood types are introduced and explained to show their relevance at a crime scene. Different biological fluids are identified, and collection techniques are described based on the circumstances of the evidence. Sexual assault collection kits are explained, and information pertaining to the contents of the kit are listed to explain what types of biological fluids can be obtained from both the victim and the suspect. The chapter ends with a laboratory exercise to show proficiency with identifying blood types and evidence collection of blood samples from a crime scene.

KEY TERMS

biological fluids
blood types
buccal swab
DNA

CASE FILE 00-123456: BLOOD TYPING AND BIOLOGICAL FLUIDS

During the search of the Ashley residence, crime scene technicians noted multiple blood stains both inside and outside of the house. The crime scene technicians at the Ashley double homicide collected multiple blood samples for further processing at the forensic laboratory. As DNA analysis will take some time for results to be delivered, blood typing was used on the evidence. The crime scene technicians swabbed the multiple stains located on the front steps of the Ashley residence.

Blood samples were collected from William and Jane Ashley at the medical examiner's office. Elimination samples from Lynette Saunders were also taken for comparison purposes back at the lab. Investigators obtained a warrant, and laboratory technicians collected blood samples from Doug Parsons, John Lee, and Antonia Sanchez.

BLOOD TYPING AND BIOLOGICAL FLUIDS

Blood Typing

Blood typing has been used for many years in forensic science and was the main source of blood determinations prior to deoxyribonucleic acid (DNA) being introduced as a more conclusive form of evidence. Four main blood types are used for identification purposes, but there are eight groups, which are more specific and relate directly to the antigen present in the blood. In addition, the basic A-antigen and B-antigen in an individual's blood will also contain the presence of an Rh factor of positive or negative.

The four blood types are:

A
B
AB
O

Once human blood is identified at a crime scene, the specific blood type can be determined. Unfortunately, this is not individualized to a specific person but helps narrow the percentage of the population that has that specific blood type. If blood typing is the only option in a case, the investigator could narrow the suspect pool by determining the blood type found at the crime scene and comparing the information to the blood type of each possible suspect.

Presumptive tests for blood can be used to determine if (1) a reddish-brown stain found at a crime scene is indeed blood or (2) blood found at a scene is human versus animal. One thing to remember with presumptive tests is that they are used to give a general idea about the source but are not an official determination. Confirmatory tests for blood are used to provide the investigator with a conclusive determination regarding the type of substance recovered at a scene or to determine whether the blood is human versus animal. Today, confirmatory tests can be more useful for later court testimony and results can be more conclusive to identify specific sources.

At the crime scene a sterile cotton swab must be used by the crime scene technician to collect potential blood for further testing. If the blood source is still wet, the cotton swab can be dipped in the blood and allowed time to air dry in a protected area. If the blood source is dry, there are two options for evidence collection. A cotton swab can be moistened with distilled water and rubbed over the dry sample. The sample area of blood can also be scraped and sealed in an envelope.

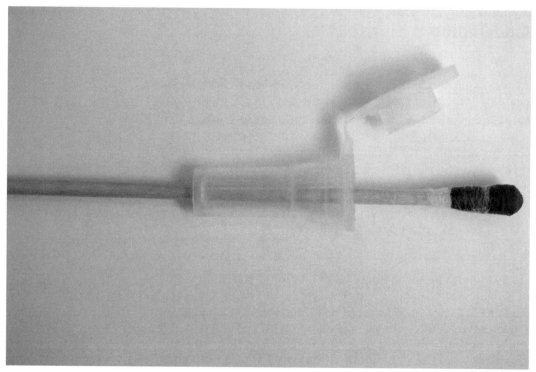

Swab of blood.

DNA

In many cases involving blood typing and DNA, elimination standards must be taken from the victim and suspect. With the assistance of a medical professional, blood can be extracted, but, more commonly, a buccal or cheek swab can be collected. A buccal swab can be taken by rubbing a sterile cotton swab on the inside of the mouth against each cheek in order to transfer skin cells to the swab.

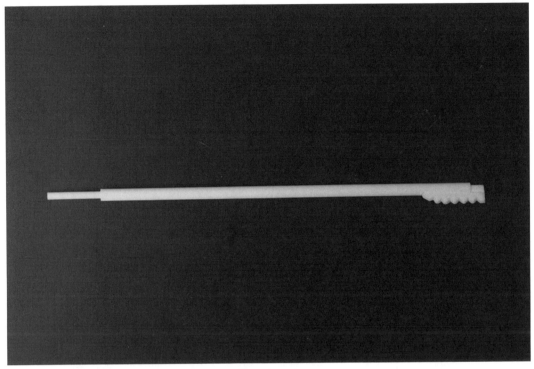

Buccal swab.

Biological Fluids

Biological fluids consist of semen, saliva, and vaginal secretions, which are used to identify sources of potential DNA and to corroborate the sequence of events at a crime scene. Many sexual offenses involve the possibility of semen and vaginal secretions as evidence. First, the stain must be located on the piece of evidence; sometimes this can be a difficult task due to the color and texture of the item. In the case of semen, the stain often can be located by looking for a stiff portion of the fabric. Chemical tests are used to both locate and identify the sample as a seminal fluid secretion. The most important requirement for seminal fluid on evidence is to identify the stain as semen so further DNA processing can be completed to determine a source.

In the case of sexual assaults, seminal fluid is not the only piece of evidence found at the scene. A sexual assault kit is used to assist with the collection, packaging, and submission of evidence at the hospital. The sexual assault kit contains instructions and packaging material in order to streamline the process and

Sexual offense collection kit.

guarantee that all relevant, required samples are collected and remain separate to avoid contamination.

The first step is to collect the clothing of the person involved in the crime. If there are possible seminal stains on the clothing, the item must be carefully folded and placed in the evidence bag to prevent any biological material from flaking off. The following

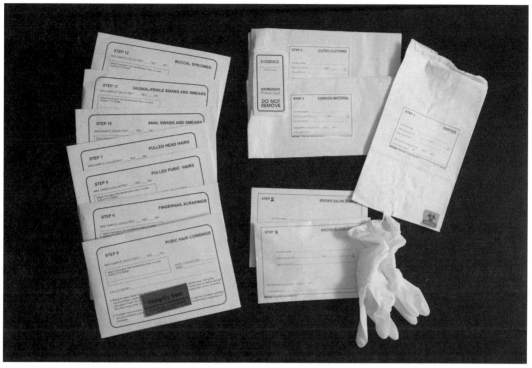

Contents of a sexual offense kit.

additional pieces of evidence are collected utilizing the material
contained within the sexual assault kit:

- Hair combings—pubic and head region
- Vaginal swabs and smears
- Anal swabs and smears
- Saliva swabs and smears
- Blood samples
- Saliva samples
- Fingernail scrapings
- Clothing—separated by individual article
- Biological fluid scrapings

PRELAB ACTIVITY REVIEW AND PRACTICE
Define the Following Terms

blood types
DNA
mitochondrial DNA
nuclear DNA

Practice Exercises

Results for the blood typing of the samples collected from the Ashley homicide have been processed. According to the forensic serologist, the following results were determined:

Blood samples recovered from the master bedroom were determined to be O+ and A−

Blood samples recovered from the footwear impressions in the upstairs hallway were determined to be B+

Blood samples from the front steps were determined to be B+

Name of sample	Blood type
William Ashley	O+
Jane Ashley	A−
Lynette Saunders	O−
Doug Parsons	B+
John Lee	O+
Antonia Sanchez	B+

	A	B
A	AA	AB
B	AB	BB

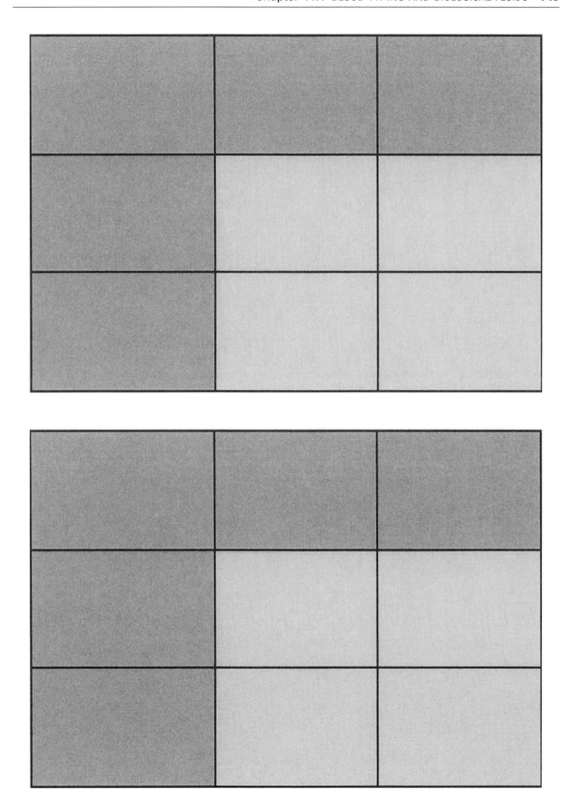

Who could have left the samples recovered from the master bedroom?

Who could have left the samples recovered from the footwear impressions in the upstairs hallway?

Who could have left the sample recovered from the front steps?

Determine the possible blood types for the soon-to-be parents.

Example:

Carrie Snell (blood type AB) and Jacob Adler (blood type B)

Sara Manchester (blood type A) and Chris Harmon (blood type O)

LABORATORY EXERCISE: BIOLOGICAL FLUIDS

CLASSROOM AND ONLINE INSTRUCTIONS

Classroom Course—If you are completing Laboratory #11 in a classroom setting, you can mix fake blood using the formula contained within the laboratory exercise or you can use blood purchased through a biological supply company for a more realistic experiment.

Online Course—If you are completing Laboratory #11 in an online course, you can make your own fake blood using the formula contained within the laboratory exercise.

Materials

- Mixing bowl
- Mixing spoon
- Water
- Corn syrup
- Red food coloring
- Corn starch
- Piece of clothing or cloth
- Cotton swabs
- Envelopes
- Clear packing tape
- Pen

Fake Blood Recipe

Needed Items

- Mixing bowl
- Metal mixing spoon
- Water
- Corn syrup
- Red food coloring
- Corn starch (optional)

Method

1. Pour corn syrup in the mixing bowl and slowly add water until the consistency is liquid enough to cause a gravitational drip.
2. If the consistency is too watery, add a small amount of corn starch, but avoid adding too much as it will cause the blood to clump.
3. Add red food coloring until the color is suitable.

1. Using the fake blood formula, mix up a small amount of fake blood.
2. Place some fake blood on the floor and allow it to dry, place some fake blood on a scrap piece of clothing, and place some fake blood on the desk.
3. Using a cotton swab, take a sample of the wet blood on the desk and allow the swab to dry. Never blow on the swab as this will cause contamination of the sample. You can set the swab aside in a safe, noncontaminated environment to dry.
4. Using a cotton swab, moisten the end of the swab with a small amount of water (should be distilled water, but plain tap water can be used for this exercise) and swab the dry sample from the floor.
5. Using a cotton swab, moisten the end of the swab and extract a dry sample from the clothing.

LABORATORY #12 BLOOD SPATTER ANALYSIS

CHAPTER OUTLINE

12.1 **Blood Spatter**
12.2 **Laboratory Exercise: Blood Spatter**

LEARNING OBJECTIVES

* Identify blood spatter
* Understand the different types of spatter analysis associated with a crime scene
* Explain low-, medium-, and high-velocity spatter
* Determine the methods used to locate the point of origin and the angle of impact of the suspect and victim
* Identify the angles of various blood stains

WHAT YOU WILL LEARN

Laboratory #12, Blood Spatter Analysis, introduces the student to various types of spatter patterns, including swipes, wipes, and transfer stains. The different aspects of spatter analysis are explained in regard to locating the samples and identifying the size, shape, and location of the blood. High-, medium-, and low-velocity spatter is explained according to the characteristics of the crime scene. Point of origin and angle of impact of each blood stain are analyzed to determine the location of the suspect and the victim. Angles of various blood stains are presented to determine the mathematical calculation to determine the point of origin. The chapter ends with a laboratory exercise to show proficiency with completing angles and low, medium, and high velocity.

KEY TERMS

angle of impact
arterial spatter
cast-off spatter

high velocity
low velocity
medium velocity
spatter analysis
swipe pattern
transfer pattern
wipe pattern

CASE FILE 00-123456: BLOOD SPATTER ANALYSIS

Multiple blood spatters and bloodstains were found at the Ashley residence during the crime scene investigation. The forensic serologist and the crime scene technicians examined the blood spatter located in the master bedroom to determine the angle of impact, the directionality, and the point of origin. Blood stains resembling footwear impressions located in the upstairs hallway were also enhanced using chemicals. The investigators determined the path of the bloody footwear impressions went from the master bedroom down the front staircase to the front door, where the impressions were so faint they could not be visualized anymore even with chemicals. This recreation of the scene using blood evidence proved the assumption that the crime occurred in the master bedroom and the suspect left the scene through the front door after the crimes were committed.

BLOOD SPATTER

Blood-spatter analysis or blood-stain pattern interpretation is used by investigators to reconstruct the crime scene to determine the sequence of events, number of impacts of the weapon to the surface, weapon characteristics, whether or not statements provided by witnesses, victims, and suspects are consistent with the scene, and to apprehend individuals responsible for committing the crime. Blood-spatter analysis takes into account the properties of blood and the principles of gravity to explain the placement of different types of blood at a crime scene. Blood is a cohesive molecule, which leaves the body and, based on velocity and gravitational pull, is moved through the air until it collides

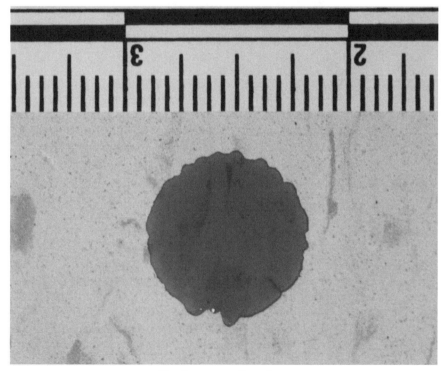

Blood on a smooth surface.

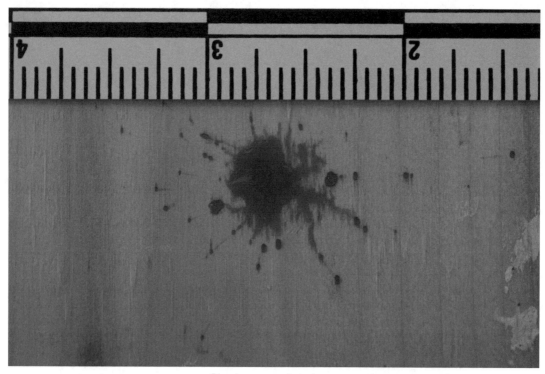

Blood on a rough surface.

with a surface, such as a wall or floor. Once the blood makes contact with a surface, the type of surface dictates the form of spatter that will be seen by the investigator. If the blood impacts a smooth textured surface, such as glass or a flat tile, there will be little spatter. If the blood impacts a rough textured surface, such as wood or corrugated tile, there will be extensive spatter.

Investigation

The shape of the stain will assist the investigator in determining the directionality of the blood as it traveled through the air; once the direction has been determined, the angle of impact or point of origin can be calculated. Blood stains that have an elongated appearance and a tail can be calculated to determine the point of origin. The tail also aids in determining the direction of travel of the stain. Think of the tail with an imaginary arrow placed on the end. This fictional arrow will point in the direction of travel of the stain, which means the stain was traveling in that direction through the air until contact with the surface occurred

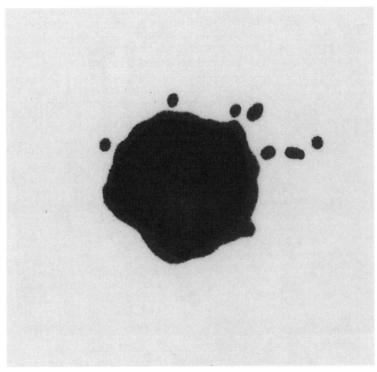

90° stain.

and stopped the motion of the stain. The opposite side of the blood-stain tail would lead to the point or origin or where the blood drop originated from.

The shape of the stain or tail is sometimes attributed to cast-off. Cast-off is where blood is on a source, such as a golf club, and once the club is swung the direction of travel will cause the blood to leave the source and impact a new location. The cast-off blood stains could be above the individual on the ceiling, behind the individual on the wall or furniture, or on the floor behind the individual.

Each elongated blood stain should be measured and calculated to determine the angle. The angle can be used to string the stain back to the point of origin or the point of convergence, which is where the weapon and suspect were in relation to the victim. If the blood stain is circular in shape, the point of origin is generally 90°, which means the width and the length are about equal in measurement. If the stain is elongated or teardrop shaped, the angle is less than 90°, which means the width and length are different in measurement. In order to calculate the angle of impact, you need to measure the width and the length of

Investigative Tip

The point of origin can help the investigator determine how many individuals or the number of impacts involved in the crime.

Greater than 90° stain.

the stain from the main portion of the stain, excluding the tail length.

Once the width and the length of the blood stain have been measured, the following formula can be used to calculate the angle:

Sin^{-1} = Width/Length

Example:

    Width = 1.5 cm

    Length = 3.0 cm

    Sin^{-1} = 1.5/3.0

    Sin^{-1} = 0.5 cm

    Angle = 30°

Each blood stain with a tail should be measured and the angle calculated. Once all of the angles have been determined, a blood spatter string can be used to locate the point of origin. String each individual stain, and use a protractor to see if one or more points of convergence exist for the crime. If more than one point of origin exists, the investigator can recreate the scenario of the scene to determine the number of impacts, the number of

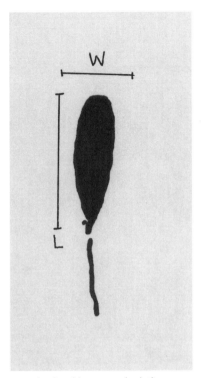

Angle of impact calculation.

suspects, or the movement of the suspect and victim throughout the scene during the commission of the crime.

Point of origin and angle of impact are not the only things derived from a blood stain at a crime scene. The following types of blood-stain interpretation can be used by an investigator to recreate the scene of the crime and determine necessary elements of the case.

Arterial staining or spurts are caused by a direct impact severing the carotid artery of the victim; while the blood is still pumping directly from the heart, a severe stain is caused by a large pressurized volume of blood leaving the body.

A swipe blood-stain pattern occurs when an object with blood comes into contact with a clean surface and a transfer or movement of the blood happens. Sometimes a swipe pattern can have a direction of travel for the stain if the person or object leaving the blood is in motion.

A transfer stain happens when a blood stain is disturbed by an object coming into contact with the surface and either leaving a distinct impression in the blood or the resulting impression is

Investigative Tip

If you do not have special blood-spatter string at a scene you can use colored string from a local hardware store or elastic yarn found at a hobby store.

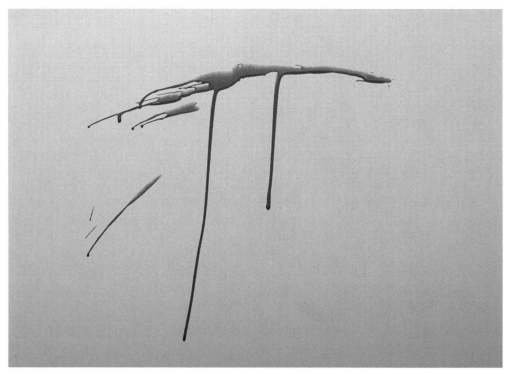

Arterial spurt.

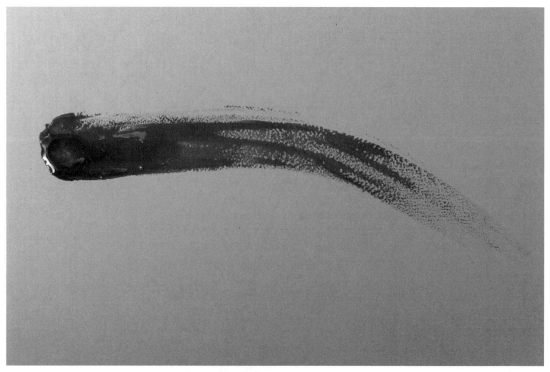

Swipe pattern.

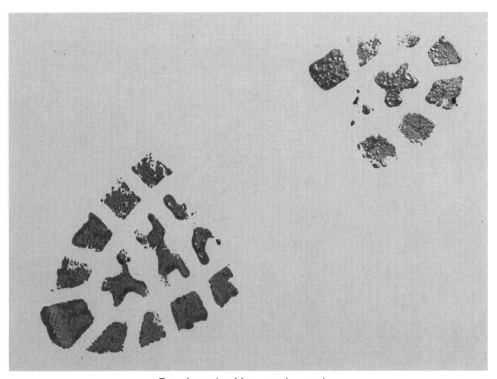

Transfer stain of footwear impression.

left visible in the blood, such as bloody footwear impressions left on the floor of a crime scene.

A wipe stain occurs when an object distorts the original pool of blood. In some instances, the wipe pattern will provide the investigator with an idea about the weapon, as the shape of the instrument can be apparent in the new impression.

Low-velocity blood stains appear as large stains with very little spatter and are caused by the dripping of blood from a source. An example of a low-velocity stain would be blood dripping from the weapon onto the floor and may appear as a 90° stain. Medium-velocity blood stains appear as spatter with directionality and tails, which are smaller in diameter than low-velocity stains. An example of a medium-velocity stain would be attributed to blunt force trauma where a weapon, such as a golf club, comes into contact with the individual. High-velocity blood stains appear as very small stains or mist with the smallest diameters when compared with low and medium velocity. An example of a high-velocity stain would be caused from a gunshot wound.

A wipe using a knife blade.

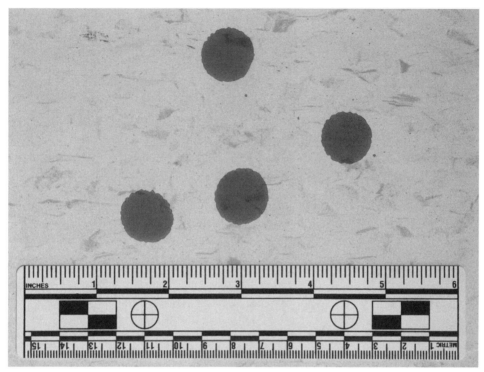

Low velocity.

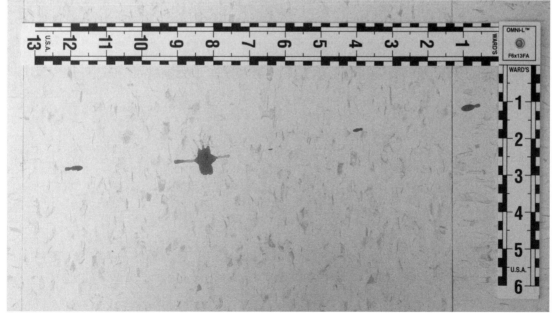

Medium velocity.

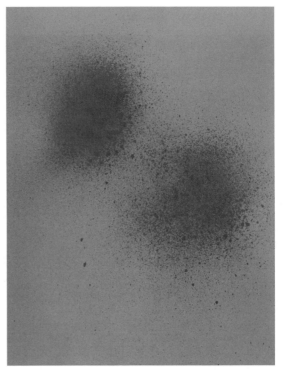

High velocity.

PRELAB ACTIVITY REVIEW AND PRACTICE
Define the Following Terms

angle of impact
arterial spatter
cast off spatter
high velocity
low velocity
medium velocity
spatter analysis
swipe pattern
transfer pattern
wipe pattern

Practice Exercises

Some of the blood spatter samples recovered from the residence are listed here.

Identify the following stain as high, medium, or low velocity and explain the potential source.

Measure the stains and determine the angle of impacts.

Explain the potential angles and recreate the scene.

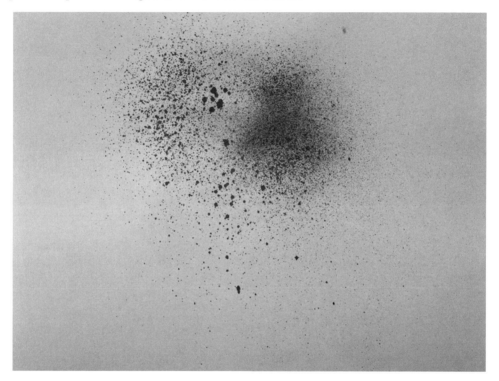

Blood stain 1.

Blood stain 2.

Blood stain 3.

Blood stain 4.

LABORATORY EXERCISE: BLOOD SPATTER

CLASSROOM AND ONLINE COURSE INSTRUCTIONS

Classroom Course—If you are completing Laboratory #12 in a classroom setting, you can mix fake blood using the formula contained within the laboratory exercise. Use butcher paper and secure it to the wall or floor for comparing blood spatter analysis. Try dropping the blood on different surfaces associated with the classroom, such as wood desks and smooth floor tiles.

Online Course—If you are completing Laboratory #12 in an online course, you can make your own fake blood using the formula contained within the laboratory exercise. Take an old sheet or towel and secure it to the wall for completing your own blood spatter analysis.

Materials

- Mixing bowl
- Mixing spoon
- Water
- Corn syrup
- Red food coloring
- Corn starch
- White cardboard or butcher paper
- Sponge
- Tool (hammer, golf club, baseball bat)
- Ruler
- Calculator (with scientific functions)
- Protractor
- Spray bottle or aerosol can
- Pen

Fake Blood Recipe

Needed Items

- Mixing bowl
- Metal mixing spoon
- Water
- Corn syrup
- Red food coloring
- Corn starch (optional)

Method

1. Pour corn syrup in a mixing bowl and slowly add water until the consistency is liquid enough to cause a gravitational drip.
2. If the consistency is too watery, add a small amount of corn starch, but avoid adding too much as it will cause the blood to clump.
3. Add red food coloring until the color is suitable.

The Exercise

1. Use either fake blood purchased through a forensic supplier or make your own fake blood using the suggested recipe.
2. Place a sheet of butcher paper or white cardboard on the wall and floor.
3. Take a household sponge and place a small amount of blood on the sponge. You can hit the bloodied sponge with a hammer, baseball bat, or golf club to recreate medium-velocity spatter.
4. Once a sufficient amount of spatter is on the butcher paper or cardboard, select at least 10 blood stains with tails.
5. Measure the stains and use the calculation for angle of impact.
6. Once the angles have been determined, use a protractor and string to determine the point of origin.
7. Place a sheet of butcher paper on the floor.
8. Take the same object used to create the medium-velocity spatter and dip it in the blood.
9. Walk across the butcher paper while holding the bloody weapon at your side. You should see blood drops on the butcher paper covering the floor, which recreates low-velocity spatter falling at a 90° angle.
10. Place a sheet of butcher paper on the wall and floor.
11. Using an empty spray bottle or empty aerosol canister, pour some of the fake blood inside. Now spray the blood at the wall to replicate high-velocity blood spatter.

13

LABORATORY #13 GLASS

CHAPTER OUTLINE
13.1 Glass
13.2 Laboratory Exercise: Glass

LEARNING OBJECTIVES
- Understand the different types of glass
- Identify samples of glass
- Explain the process to determine the sequence of glass damage attributed to gun shots
- Explain the types of cracks and how this can be used for analysis
- Examine fracture matches to reconstruct broken glass
- Comprehend the required crime scene paperwork

WHAT YOU WILL LEARN

Laboratory #13, Glass, introduces the student to various techniques for identifying the specific type of glass found at a crime scene. The various types of cracks, such as concentric and radial, are explained to assist the investigator with determining the sequence of damage attributed to gun shots. The direction of breakage through glass can also be identified to assist with reconstruction of the crime scene. The chapter ends with a laboratory exercise to show proficiency in completing fracture matches of glass analysis and completion of required paperwork.

KEY TERMS
concentric crack
conchoidal lines
radial crack

CASE FILE 00-123456: GLASS

The crime scene technicians processed the Ashley residence and discovered a broken rear glass door of the house and glass fragments located in the back alley behind the Ashley property. The glass fragments located in the back alley were found under magnification to have a light green tint, which is consistent with a bottle used to package alcohol. Glass located on the kitchen floor was consistent with the remaining glass fragments still attached to the door frame. The glass was also located on the inside of the residence, which is consistent with the assumption that the suspect broke the window from the outside in order to gain access to the house.

The crime scene technicians also noticed the master bedroom window had three holes consistent with bullets traveling through glass from the inside of the house to the outside of the house. The three holes in the glass were consistent with some of the cartridge casings located on the master bedroom floor.

GLASS

Glass analysis is a form of trace evidence that can be recovered from a crime scene or from a suspect that can tie the individual to the scene and the victim. Glass evidence can assist the investigator with locating the source of the sample and includes glass found in windows, car windshields, bottles, headlights, light bulbs, and eye glasses. When glass is recovered at a crime scene, the source of the evidence can sometimes be identified easily simply by observing the main properties of glass and the shape of the sample. If the glass is found shattered at a scene in small cubes it can be reasonably assumed that the sample originated as tempered glass found in automobile side and rear windows.

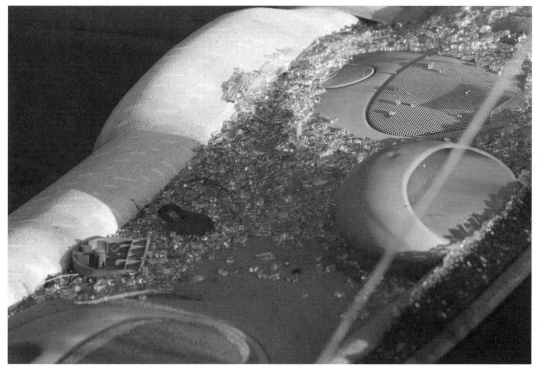

Shattered glass.

If the glass recovered at a crime scene is found in large jagged pieces it can be reasonably assumed that the sample originated from a window—not associated with an automobile. The color of the glass sample can also be important for determining the source of a sample, as brown glass may be indicative of glass used for beer bottles or multicolor glass may indicate a stained glass window in a house or church.

Glass analysis can also be used to determine the entry/exit location for a burglary if a household window is found broken or the sequence of bullet holes in an automobile windshield. Shards of glass found in a house can assist an investigator with determining whether the glass was broken from the outside to the inside or from the inside to the outside. This could be a crucial piece of evidence if there was a possibility of a staged crime scene.

Glass shattered by a bullet.

PRELAB ACTIVITY REVIEW AND PRACTICE

Define the Following Terms

concentric crack
conchoidal lines
radial crack

Practice Exercise

Compare the piece of window glass containing three bullet holes and determine the sequence of shots. Label the three holes with first contact shot, second contact shot, and third contact shot.

LABORATORY EXERCISE: GLASS

CLASSROOM AND ONLINE INSTRUCTIONS

Classroom Course—If you are completing Laboratory #13 in a classroom setting, you can use a bottle placed in a paper bag as a sample for the laboratory exercise. If you have access to other types of glass, such as tempered, you should be able to analyze the marks on the side of the glass in order to determine the direction of breakage.

Online Course—If you are completing Laboratory #13 in an online course, you can use a beer bottle as a sample for the laboratory exercise. You can also use broken pieces of glass at your home to compare the similarities and differences.

Materials

- Glass bottle
- Paper bags
- Clear tape
- Pen

The Exercise

1. Take an empty glass drink bottle and place it in a paper bag. Gently break the bottle in the paper bag. Be careful not to cut yourself!
2. Carefully remove the pieces of glass and, using clear tape, reconstruct the bottle.
3. Obtain a piece of glass-related evidence, such as eye glasses, and package the evidence to prevent damage during transport to the laboratory. Label the packaging with the following information:
   - Case number
   - Date/time
   - Explanation of sample, that is, glass from living room floor
   - Names of person collecting the sample

4. Once the packaging is labeled, seal the packaging with clear packing tape or evidence processing tape. Place your initials, date/time, and case number on the seal. You can refer back to the laboratory activity pertaining to evidence packaging.

5. Using a blank evidence submission form located in the appendix, complete one submission form detailing the evidence.

6. Using a blank chain of custody form, complete one chain of custody form detailing transportation from the scene to the evidence locker.

14

LABORATORY #14 HAIR AND FIBER

CHAPTER OUTLINE
14.1 Hair and Fiber
14.2 Laboratory Exercise: Hair and Fiber

LEARNING OBJECTIVES
- Identify human hair versus animal hair
- Identify natural fibers versus synthetic fibers
- Explain the three layers of hair
- Understand the properties of hair and fiber analysis in a forensic setting
- Demonstrate evidence collection techniques for hair and fiber collection
- Comprehend the required crime scene paperwork

WHAT YOU WILL LEARN

Laboratory #14, Hair and Fiber, introduces the student to various principles associated with the forensic value of hair and fiber evidence. The characteristics of human hair versus animal hair and natural fibers versus synthetic fibers are addressed. The three layers of hair are explained to understand the importance and forensic value of each layer. Evidence collection of hairs and fibers is presented to demonstrate the various techniques used depending on the surface of the sample. The chapter ends with a laboratory exercise to show proficiency with evidence collection of hairs and fibers, as well as packaging techniques used for trace evidence.

KEY TERMS
cortex
cuticle
medulla
natural fiber
synthetic fiber

CASE FILE 00-123456: HAIR AND FIBER

Crime scene technicians processed the entire Ashley residence and found multiple hairs and fibers located throughout the scene. The hairs and fibers were collected from both the scene and the bodies of William and Jane Ashley using trace tape and packaged for further processing. The samples were narrowed down to hairs from humans and animals, plus fibers attributed to natural and man-made sources.

Twelve hairs were identified as short gray hairs consistent with the size, shape, and color of William Ashley's hair. Twenty-six hairs were identified as long brown hair consistent with the size, shape, and color of Jane Ashley's hair.

Roughly 100 hairs were identified as originating from a canine, and about half were consistent with the size, shape, and color of Muffin, the Pekinese's hair. The remaining hairs were compared to samples collected from a dog bed used by Gracie, the Chihuahua. The remaining hairs were consistent with the size, shape, and color of Gracie's hair.

Five hairs and two fibers remained from evidence collected from the Ashley double homicide and were not identified with either of the two victims or the two dogs.

HAIR AND FIBER

Trace evidence is a forensic science discipline, which mainly comprises hairs and fibers recovered from a crime scene but can also include glass and paint analysis, soil identification, and footwear comparisons. Hair analysis is the most common form of trace evidence recovered at a crime scene; however, hair as a forensic investigative tool cannot be identified to a single source or one specific individual. Comparison results can provide descriptive information regarding the length, color, and texture, but the information is generalized to a large portion of the population.

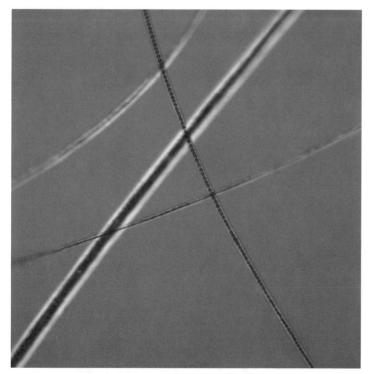

Cat hair under a microscope. iStockphoto.

Hair analysis requires examination of the three components of hair: cuticle, cortex, and medulla. The cuticle, the outer portion of the hair forming a scaled shell, can be used to understand attributes of the hair, but, most importantly, the cuticle can assist the forensic scientist with species identification. The cortex is the middle layer of the hair shaft and provides the greatest forensic importance as it contains the color of the specific strand of hair. The medulla, or center of the hair shaft, varies between individuals and specific hair strands. The forensic value of the medulla can assist the trace examiner with determining the type of hair in relation to racial origins and whether it is human versus animal. In order for hair evidence collected at a crime scene to be used for individualization purposes, a follicular tag or skin tag must be present on the hair sample. The follicular tag contains DNA when the hair is pulled from the root, and the DNA can be analyzed and used for individual identification.

Fiber analysis can be used to determine the source and origin of fibers recovered at crime scenes and can narrow the field into two different classifications: natural and manufactured. Natural

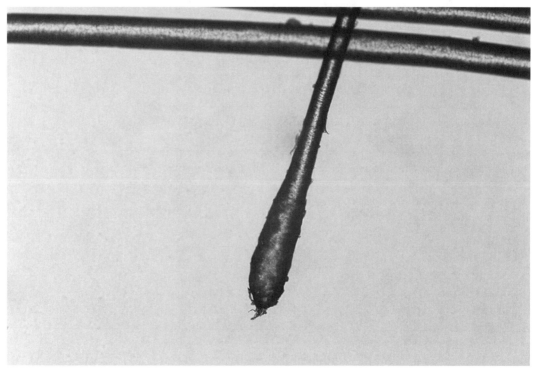

Hair root. iStockphoto.

Dust under a microscope. iStockphoto.

fibers come from animal or plant sources found in nature and include cotton, wool, cashmere, and alpaca. Synthetic fibers are man-made and manufactured from chemical components in a factory and include nylon, acrylic, and polyester. The comparison of both natural and synthetic fibers is similar to hair comparisons, where the samples are examined under a microscope to observe the size and shape of the sample. When analyzing fiber evidence recovered from a crime scene, a chemical composition test must also be performed in order to identify the origin of the sample. Evidence collection of hair and fibers found at a crime scene can be accomplished different ways depending on where the sample is located. If the possible hair or fiber is located on a victim, the sample can be recovered during examination at the hospital, morgue, or crime scene. The evidence can be collected using tweezers and placed in an envelope or in a folded sheet of paper. Hair and fiber evidence can also be collected using a piece of sterile trace tape or an adhesive lifter placed over the sample and then secured in an envelope.

Fibers.

PRELAB ACTIVITY REVIEW AND PRACTICE

Define the Following Terms

cortex
cuticle
medulla
natural fiber
synthetic fiber

Practice Exercise

Label the three layers of hair.

Hairs found at the Ashley double homicide were all human and, upon comparison, were linked back to Lynette Saunders, Antonia Sanchez, and Doug Parsons. Assume you are viewing a human head hair under a microscope and draw a picture of the sample.

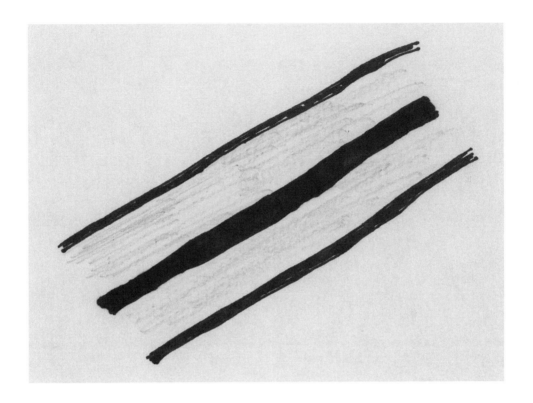

14.2

LABORATORY EXERCISE:
HAIR AND FIBER

CLASSROOM AND ONLINE INSTRUCTIONS

Classroom Course—If you are completing Laboratory #14 in a classroom setting, you can compare multiple samples of hairs and fibers using a microscope. Place individual hairs under a microscope and see if the medulla is visible. If so, sketch it and then compare all of the samples to determine human versus animal.

Online Course—If you are completing Laboratory #14 in an online course, you can use a piece of packing tape and create a tape lift for your clothing. See how many hairs and fibers you can identify based simply on appearance. Take samples from known sources, such as your dog or cat, for comparison purposes.

Materials

- Clear packing tape
- Piece of clothing (clothing is not damaged or destroyed by lab)
- Transparency paper or overlay paper
- Handheld magnifier or microscope
- Paper bag
- Pen

The Exercise

1. Using a piece of clear packing tape, place the adhesive side on a piece of clothing and attempt to collect both hairs and fibers. If you have a pet, such as a dog or cat, use an article of clothing containing animal hairs.
2. If you have a sheet of transparency paper you can place the tape on clear paper to view the hairs and fibers. If you do not have transparency paper, you can fold a piece of tape together to view the samples.

3. Using a handheld magnifier or microscope, view the hairs and fibers. Describe the different types of strands. Can you distinguish between human and animal hairs and natural and synthetic fibers?

4. Select at least two hairs and two fibers and sketch the layers of the strands.

5. You should now have at least one tape lift. Place the tape lift in a brown paper bag or in an envelope and label the packaging with the following information:
   - Case number
   - Date/time
   - Location of tape lift
   - Explanation of sample, that is, tape lift recovered from sweater belonging to
   - Name of person collecting the sample

6. Once the paper bag or envelope is labeled, seal it (DO NOT use saliva because this can contaminate the sample!) with clear packing tape or evidence processing tape. Place your initials, date/time, and case number on the seal. You can refer back to the laboratory activity pertaining to evidence packaging.

7. Using the evidence submission form located in the appendix, complete a submission form describing the trace evidence sample.

8. Using the chain of custody form located in the appendix, complete a chain of custody form to track the evidence from the crime scene to the trial.

15

LABORATORY #15 DRUGS AND TOXICOLOGY

CHAPTER OUTLINE

15.1 Drug Chemistry
15.2 Laboratory Exercise: Toxicology

LEARNING OBJECTIVES

- Identify drug-related evidence
- Explain the importance of descriptions associated with packaging drug evidence
- Describe the instruments of analysis used for drug and toxicology testing
- Understand the difference between presumptive and confirmatory tests
- Explain the uses of toxicological analysis in forensic science
- Identify the blood alcohol concentration
- Comprehend the required crime scene paperwork

WHAT YOU WILL LEARN

Laboratory #15, Drugs and Toxicology, introduces the student to various techniques for identifying and documenting drug-related evidence. Instruments of analysis for processing samples of drug and toxicology evidence are explained to differentiate between presumptive and confirmatory tests. The use of forensic toxicology is explained based on crime scene evidence and items of interest, such as stomach contents, from a victim. Blood alcohol concentrations (BAC) are also explained, and the formula for analysis is included with examples. The chapter ends with a laboratory exercise to show proficiency with BAC calculations, drug evidence descriptions, and completion of required paperwork.

KEY TERMS

blood alcohol concentration
gas chromatography/mass spectrometry
scheduling of drugs
toxicology analysis

CASE FILE 00-123456: DRUGS AND TOXICOLOGY

The crime scene technicians processed the entire Ashley residence and found three empty pill bottles in the upstairs hallway on the floor. Two of the bottles were labeled with prescriptions for sleeping aids and migraine medicine for Jane Ashley. The third bottle was labeled with a prescription for Oxycodone for William Ashley. One pill bottle containing eight small blue tablets was located outside the Ashley residence in the bushes. The pill bottle was labeled as a prescription for blood pressure medication for William Ashley.

Crime scene technicians also photographed and collected a small plastic bag containing a white powdery substance from the front hallway floor. It was assumed that the white powdery substance was cocaine, so the evidence was submitted to the crime laboratory for confirmation.

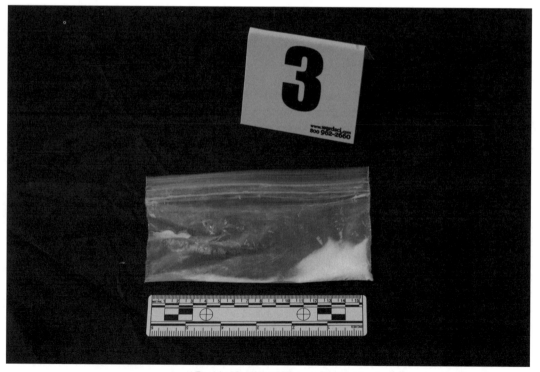

Powder found at crime scene.

DRUG CHEMISTRY

Introduction

Drug chemists are responsible for the analysis of unknown substances recovered from a crime scene to determine whether they contain a controlled substance or drug. When unknown, potentially illegal substances are recovered from scenes, the drug analysis unit at a crime laboratory is responsible for determining how much of the substance is present, what the substance is, and possibly the purity and/or form of the substance. Typically the first step in the analysis is to obtain an

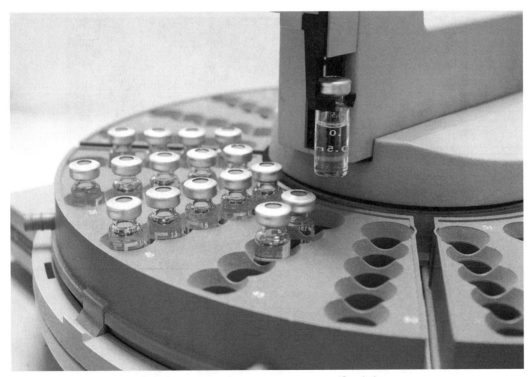

Gas chromatography mass spectrometer. iStockphoto.

accurate weight of the sample separate from whatever packaging the substance arrived in. The next step would be a color test to guide the analyst and then finally some type of instrumentation to confirm the substance. Gas chromatography mass spectrometry (GC-MS) is a valuable tool for separating out the different parts in a mixture, such as an actual drug and a cutting agent. Fourier transform infrared spectroscopy (FTIR) can be used to determine the form of the drug [cocaine base (crack) or cocaine hydrochloride].

Investigation

Frequently an analyst will also be asked to examine drug paraphernalia for possible residue. Examples of items that typically contain residue could include digital scales, plastic bags, spoons, and syringes. All of these items may contain residues of controlled substances, which could be beneficial information to the investigation.

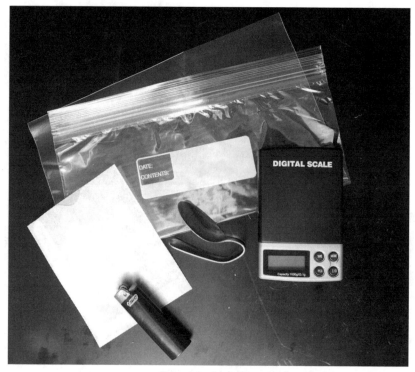

Drug paraphernalia.

Prescription Drugs

Drug chemistry does not always deal with illegal substances, such as marijuana and cocaine, but the division can also analyze prescription medicine used outside of the recommended capacity by unauthorized users. In recent years, new designer or synthetic drugs have become more prevalent in the drug community, which means that scientists must stay abreast of new trends and products available to the public. If a new drug is introduced to the United States market, the drug chemist must be able to identify the chemical components to determine if the substance is controlled.

Role of Toxicologist

Toxicologists work in conjunction with the medical examiner's office and the forensic laboratory depending on the location of the unit. The toxicology division is responsible for analyzing substances for the detection of poisons or foreign components that may be present in the body. Similar to the drug unit, this can be accomplished using GC-MS. Forensic toxicologists can receive samples of blood and urine to determine if alcohol or drugs are in the body and if the level could have contributed to death.

Stomach Contents

Toxicologists also analyze stomach contents received from the medical examiner's office to determine if poison is present in the gastric juices or the types of food particles remaining in the stomach after a meal for assistance with time-of-death determinations. The toxicology unit does not always analyze samples of deceased individuals. In many instances, the samples from blood and urine received from police departments are recovered from people who have been arrested for driving under the influence or for employment screening purposes.

PRELAB ACTIVITY REVIEW AND PRACTICE
Define the Following Terms

BAC
GC-MS
scheduling of drugs
toxicology analysis

Blood Alcohol Concentration Formula

BAC = [(standard drinks × 0.06)(100 × 1.055)/(weight × gender constant)] − [(0.015 × hours)]
- Standard drinks = alcoholic beverage = one beer (12 oz), one glass of wine (5 oz), or one shot (1.5 oz)
- 0.06 = 6% alcohol
- 100 × 1.055 = gravity of blood
- Weight = weight in pounds (lb.)
- Gender constant = 0.75, male and 0.66, female
- Hour = hours since last drink

Example: Calculate the below BAC
The victim is a 160-lb. male who consumed three beers 4 hours ago.
Standard drinks = 3 beers = 12(3) = 36
Weight = 160
Gender constant = 0.75
Hours = 4
Standard drink (0.06) = (36)(0.06) = 2.16
(100)(1.055) = 105.5
(2.16)(105.5) = 227.88
Weight (160)
Gender constant (0.75)
(160)(0.75) = 120
227.88/120 = 1.90
(0.015)(4 hours) = 0.06
1.90 − 0.06 = 1.84 BAC

Practice Exercises

Investigators spoke with friends and relatives of the Ashleys to determine their movements prior to the homicide. It was determined that the couple had been at a benefit dinner the evening before the homicide and both victims consumed alcohol. Calculate the blood alcohol concentration for William and Jane Ashley based on the following witness statements:

William Ashley, 175 lb., seven glasses of wine, 10 hours ago
Jane Ashley, 123 lb., four glasses of wine, 10 hours ago

15.2

LABORATORY EXERCISE: TOXICOLOGY

CLASSROOM AND ONLINE INSTRUCTIONS

Classroom Course—If you are completing Laboratory #15 in a classroom setting, you can analyze the scheduling of drugs and, based on information regarding specific drugs, practice describing the potential evidence in detail. Get in the habit of using descriptions rather than assumptions about the identification of a substance.

Online Course—If you are completing Laboratory #15 in an online course, you can calculate the BAC of an individual over the age of 21 who you know was drinking. Try to be as accurate as possible with the weight, number of drinks, and time since drinking.

Materials

- Pen
- Paper
- Evidence form
- Chain of custody form

The Exercise

1. Calculate the BAC for two recent arrestees: Joseph Baker and Monica Dunbar
   Joseph Baker, 180 lb., six beers, 5 hours ago
   Monica Dunbar, 125 lb., three glasses of wine, 5 hours ago
2. Using the blank evidence submission form located in the appendix, complete a submission form and describe the drug evidence listed below.
3. Using the blank chain of custody form located in the appendix, complete a chain of custody form to track the drug evidence from the crime scene to trial.

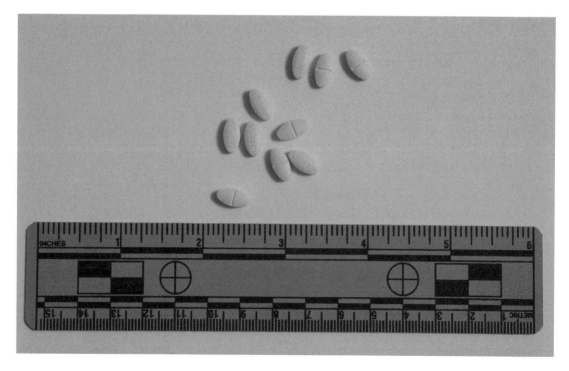

LABORATORY #16 DIGITAL FORENSICS

CHAPTER OUTLINE
16.1 **Digital Forensics**
16.2 **Laboratory Exercise: Digital Forensics**

LEARNING OBJECTIVES

* Identify electronic devices
* Understand the uses of electronic devices in the forensic setting
* Explain the evidence packing and photographic techniques at a crime scene
* Understand the components associated with electronic devices
* Comprehend the required crime scene paperwork

WHAT YOU WILL LEARN

Laboratory #16, Digital Forensics, introduces the student to various forms of electronic evidence. Electronic devices and the different components of external evidence are explained to illustrate the different items that can be retrieved at the forensic laboratory. Packaging of digital evidence is explained with photographic techniques to prevent destruction of files due to deletion or static. The chapter ends with a laboratory exercise to show proficiency in analyzing data retrieved from an electronic device and completion of required paperwork.

KEY TERMS

antistatic bag
electronic device
external drive
hard drive

CASE FILE 00-123456: DIGITAL FORENSICS

Investigators requested from the phone company copies of William and Jane Ashley's cell phone logs. A warrant was issued for copies of the phone logs for cell phones from the three possible suspects (Doug Parsons, John Lee, and Antonia Sanchez). One computer and two tablets were recovered from the office in the Ashley residence and were presumed to belong to the victims. Antonia Sanchez explained that her boss, Jane Ashley, always had her cell phone and tablet with her throughout the day. When she was at home both items were stored in the home office.

Police investigators figured the digital evidence, specifically the phone records, could be used to prove or disprove the statements provided by all people involved in the scene. This supporting information could be used as the final clue in determining the suspect of the double homicide.

DIGITAL FORENSICS

Introduction

Digital forensics is a relatively new discipline dealing with the analysis of data contained within electronic devices. In the past, digital forensics was typically a department within the police department. With the advent of new electronic devices and a decrease in cost, many people now own some type of digital product, such as a computer, tablet, or cell phone.

Smartphone.

Investigation

Digital forensic analysts acquire electronic devices recovered from crime scenes to interpret the stored and deleted information to locate a pattern of abuse or illicit behavior. When a crime scene technician uncovers electronic devices at a scene, a different technique for evidence collection is used. Electronic devices can have imbedded deletion programs, and extra measures must be taken to prevent the destruction of potential evidence.

Photographing the Evidence

When a crime scene technician encounters digital forensics, the scene should be photographed to illustrate the original setup of all evidence prior to collection. This can assist the forensic scientist at the laboratory when the equipment is analyzed and possibly reconnected.

Investigative Tip

Always take a photograph of the screen of each electronic device, especially computer monitors. In case that evidence is destroyed, the photograph can help depict the information on the machine at the time of collection.

Photographing computer evidence.

Packaging Evidence

Once the electronic devices have been photographed and sketched, each individual piece of evidence must be collected for further processing back at the laboratory. Items associated with the main piece of electronic data should be collected. This can

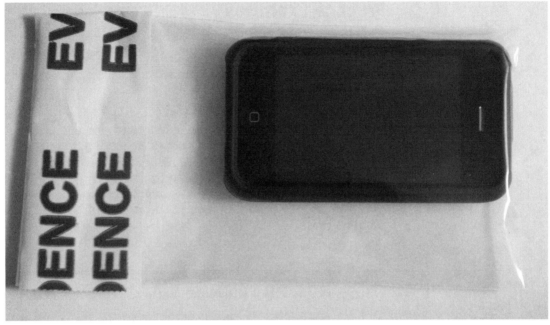

Packaged digital evidence.

include power cords, external hard drives, CDs, and flash drives. All potential evidence should be collected to avoid damage to the internal network and transported to the digital forensics unit at the crime laboratory. In some cases, typical types of forensic processing, such as fingerprints and DNA, are not requested in order to prevent chemical damage to the items.

Evidence packaging should concentrate on securing the device to avoid movement and possible damage. Boxes and large evidence bags can be used to package electronic devices. However, the internal memory of an electronic device can be destroyed by static, which is caused by placing an item in a typical plastic evidence storage bag. Specific antistatic evidence processing bags exist to package electronic devices and should be used in cases where there is cause to believe static could destroy potential evidence.

PRELAB ACTIVITY REVIEW AND PRACTICE
Define the Following Terms

antistatic bag
electronic device
external drive
hard drive

Practice Exercises

Police received the phone logs for the three possible suspects and needed to confirm information supplied by Doug Parsons, Antonia Sanchez, and John Lee.

Important Case Phone Number

John Lee explained to investigators that he could not have been responsible for the double homicide as he was talking to friends and then called his parents overseas during the homicide. Look over John Lee's cell phone records and determine if the cell phone was in use during the suspected time of death (11:00 pm–3:00 am). List the numbers called, numbers received, and duration of the calls.

JOHN LEE'S CELL PHONE RECORDS

9:09 pm—call received from (212)555-0121, duration of call 19 minutes

9:28 pm, text message received from (212)555-9273

9:29 pm, text message sent (212)555-9273

9:31 pm, text message received from (212)555-9273

9:33 pm, text message sent (212)555-9273

9:35 pm—call made to (212)555-4473, duration of call 4 minutes

10:01 pm, text message received from (212)555-9273

10:02 pm, text message sent to (212)555-9273

10:10 pm—call received from (212)555-0034, duration of call 1.5 minutes

10:14 pm—call made to (212)555-0034, duration of call 3 minutes

10:20 pm, text message received from (212)555-0034

10:22 pm, text message sent to (212)555-0034

10:46 pm—call made to (212)555-4486, duration of call 13 minutes

11:18 pm—call made to (212)555-8624, duration of call 5 minutes

11:26 pm, text message sent to (212)555-9273

11:27 pm, text message received from (212)555-9273

11:29 pm—call made to (212)555-2398, duration of call 30 seconds

12:09 am—text message received from (212)555-9273

12:45 am—call made to 011+55+(3)53987, duration of call 1 hour and 36 minutes

---

Antonia Sanchez explained to the investigators that she spoke with her boyfriend and then went to bed since she was due to pick up some items for Jane Ashley first thing in the morning. She was awoken a little after 11:00 pm by Jane Ashley calling to confirm that she would pick up her new clothes in the morning and then bring them to the house Monday morning. Look over Antonia Sanchez's cell phone records and determine if her cell phone records correspond to the statement she provided to the police. List the number called, the number received, and the duration of the calls.

ANTONIA SANCHEZ'S CELL PHONE RECORD

9:58 pm—call made to (212)555-6328, duration of call 27 minutes

10:31 pm, text message sent to (212)555-9810

11:07 pm—call received from (212)555-9810, duration of call 11 minutes

Doug Parsons explained to investigators that the last call made on his cell phone was around 6:30 pm to order a pizza. Otherwise, he was alone all evening and could not verify his whereabouts through his cell phone records. Investigators requested his cell phone records to verify his explanation; however, upon inspection, one outgoing call made at 7:03 pm could not be explained by Doug Parson's story.

DOUG PARSON'S CELL PHONE RECORDS

6:34 pm—call made to (212)555-8623, duration of call 3 minutes

7:03 pm—call made to (516)555-4340, duration of call 7 minutes

LABORATORY EXERCISE:
DIGITAL FORENSICS

CLASSROOM AND ONLINE INSTRUCTIONS

Classroom Course—If you are completing Laboratory #16 in a classroom setting, you can practice describing another classmate's digital equipment. Try to list all of the possible scenarios for why digital evidence would be used in a case.

Online Course—If you are completing Laboratory #16 in an online course, you can save and then delete a document. See if you are able to locate the copy of the document on the computer. This can also work if you print a document and then delete it.

Materials

- Electronic device (cell phone—item will not be damaged or destroyed by lab)
- Pen
- Paper

The Exercise

1. List all incoming and outgoing phone calls from your personal cell phone logs for the last 6 hours. Identify any patterns of phone calls that could be used for investigative purposes.
2. List all incoming and outgoing text messages from your personal cell phone logs for the last 6 hours. Identify any patterns of text messages that could be used for investigative purposes.
3. Assume you were questioned by your professor regarding your whereabouts when an assignment was submitted online last

night around 10:00 pm. Using your cell phone, document any information that could be used to verify your location and actions. Remember that you can use all applications installed on the phone (phone logs, text messages, Facebook, GPS, etc.).

LABORATORY #17 THE TRIAL

CHAPTER OUTLINE
17.1 The Trial
17.2 Laboratory Exercise: The Trial

LEARNING OBJECTIVES
- Comprehend the steps of a criminal trial
- Understand the forensic evidence used at trial
- Explain the importance of an expert witness
- Identify the different forms of evidence at trial

WHAT YOU WILLL LEARN

Laboratory #17, The Trial, introduces the student to the final step within the investigative process. Paperwork used from the previous 16 labs is compiled to illustrate how each forensic discipline works together to form a case and assist the investigator and legal staff. The different forms of evidence used at a trial are explained with examples. Information pertaining to the questions used during expert witness qualification and direct and cross examination is identified. The chapter ends with a laboratory exercise to show proficiency with compiling paperwork from past labs and developing a series of questions to qualify as an expert witness.

KEY TERMS
cross examination
demonstrative evidence
direct examination
expert witness
forensic science
physical evidence
testimonial evidence

CASE FILE 00-123456: INDICTMENT AND TRIAL

Investigators used all of the information from the crime scene, including the photos and the evidence, to determine the suspect. The grand jury was presented with the case information and granted an indictment. It is trial time, and each person responsible for an aspect of the case, such as the first responding officer, the investigator, the crime scene technician, and the forensic scientist, has prepared the case information for trial.

THE TRIAL

Introduction

The trial is the final stage of the case, when all of the evidence, photographs, sketches, lab reports, and identifications are compiled to assist the prosecutor with assigning charges and preparing for trial. Each of the steps involved with forensic processing is necessary; however, if the reports are not written properly, they cannot be used at trial. At the trial stage, you move from a forensic scientist or crime scene technician to an expert witness who must provide testimony in a courtroom in front of a judge and jury.

Preparation

Make a First Impression on the Jury

Before you testify at trial, there are a few things to consider since you will be qualified as an expert witness for the case. You only have a few moments when walking into the courtroom to make a first impression on the judge and jury. It is suggested that you dress professionally based on your agency preference. If you are a sworn officer, some departments require the witness to wear the uniform associated with the job. If you are a civilian employee or one without a uniform, departments typically recommend a dark-colored suit, such as blue or black, with minimal jewelry.

Go Through Your Case File and Be Thoroughly Prepared

Prior to being called to the stand, make sure you read through your case file and update yourself on the facts of the case. It is imperative that you are prepared for trial so that you can answer questions asked by the prosecutor, defense, and/or judge. If for some reason you cannot answer a question because you do not remember the facts of the case, never guess. You can always answer with "I do not remember" or "I do not know."

Testifying

Preliminary Questions

The first set of questions you will be asked at the trial are in regard to your name and background in the field you are testifying to. The series of questions pertaining to educational level, years in the field, amount of times previously testified, and total number of identifications made in the past are considered qualifying questions to prove you should be considered an expert witness.

Expert Testimony

Once you are accepted by the court as an expert witness, the second set of questions pertains specifically to the evidence and comparisons completed in the case. The prosecutor or defense (depending on who you are a witness for) will ask about recognition of the evidence, types of processing used to uncover details for the comparison, the actual comparison, and results. You may have identified the item of evidence with an individual or an object, rejected the evidence to a person or object, or determined that the sample was too small or damaged and an identification could not be concluded.

PRELAB ACTIVITY REVIEW AND PRACTICE
Define the Following Terms

cross examination
demonstrative evidence
direct examination
expert witness
forensic science
physical evidence
testimonial evidence

Practice Exercises

You have just received a subpoena requesting your testimony at the homicide trial for William and Jane Ashley.

Investigative Tip

Practice answering questions with a person who is unaware of forensic science techniques to make sure your answers make sense and are clearly articulated. You can also answer questions in front of a mirror to gauge your reaction and eye contact with jury members.

1. Compile all of the reports generated from past laboratory exercises and reread to update yourself on the results from each test.
2. List all of the relevant case facts.
3. Who is the murderer and why?

17.2

LABORATORY EXERCISE:
THE TRIAL

CLASSROOM AND ONLINE INSTRUCTIONS

Classroom Course—If you are completing Laboratory #17 in a classroom setting, write out a series of questions regarding your current course. Select a partner and position your seat so that you are facing him or her (similar to a witness stand and jury box courtroom placement). Answer the questions and analyze how you present the information. Is the information clear and understandable?

Online Course—If you are completing Laboratory #17 in an online course, write out a series of questions regarding your program of study. Answer the questions in front of a mirror. Analyze your answers, facial expressions, and head movements. Is there anything you could change?

Materials

- Pen
- Paper

The Exercise

1. Prepare your testimony by answering the following questions, which will more than likely be asked by the prosecutor or defense in order to qualify you as an expert witness.
   A. Please state your full name for the court and spell your last name.
   B. Where are you currently enrolled as a student and in what program?
   C. How long have you been a student at this institution?
   D. Briefly explain the crime scene sketches used for this case.
   E. Briefly describe the photographs taken for this case.
   F. Explain the fingerprint evidence recovered at the scene and the results of the comparisons.

G. Explain the questioned document evidence recovered at the scene, tests used, and results of the comparisons.

H. Explain the footwear impression evidence recovered at the scene and the results of the comparison.

I. Explain the tool mark evidence found at the scene and the results of the comparison.

J. Explain the blood evidence found at the scene and the results of the comparison.

K. Explain the blood spatter evidence and the results of your analysis.

L. Explain the drug and toxicology evidence recovered at the scene and the results of the analysis.

M. Explain the glass fragments recovered at the scene and the results from the tests.

N. Explain the hair and fiber evidence recovered at the scene and the results from the comparison.

O. Explain the types of evidence used for digital forensics and the results of the analysis.

P. Explain who the evidence has to and your theory of the crime scenario.

REFERENCES

Kie, Greg, SUNY Canton—Photographs, except where otherwise noted.

Saferstein R. Criminalistics: An Introduction to Forensic Science. Boston, MA: Pearson; 2011.

Stuart JH, Kish PE, Sutton TP. Principles of Bloodstain Pattern Analysis: Theory and Practice. Boca Raton, FL: CRC Press; 2005.

Wilson, Jennifer, Onondaga County Center for Forensic Sciences, Forensic Drug Chemist.

Wisbey, Dwayne, Onondaga County Sheriff's Deputy, Forensic Document Examiner.

APPENDIX: BLANK FORMS FOR EXERCISES

Incident Report		Case #	Page Number
Student's Name:		Date	Time:

Description of Incident

Incident report.

EVIDENCE COLLECTION FORM	Case #		
TYPE OF CRIME	DATE / TIME	REPORT COMPLETED BY	

PROPERTY STATUS:

☐ Evidence   ☐ Recovered   ☐ Stolen   ☐ Found   ☐ Safekeeping   ☐ Hold (Unit):   ☐ Other:

Name (If Known)	Sex Race DOB	Address	Phone
Victim:			
Suspect:			

Item Number	Quantity	Describe Items (Use as much detail as possible)

Place the Item Number(s)From Above to designate the Examination Requested: Checkbox if additional items are on an additional form: ☐

Document Examination	Drug Chemistry	Digital Evidence	Toxicology
Tool Marks	Hairs and Fibers	Fingerprints	Footwear/Tire Impressions
Glass	Biology (Blood Typing, DNA)	Documents	Other

Narrative/Notes:

Evidence collection form.

CHAIN OF CUSTODY FORM			CASE #		
Chain of Custody					
ITEM NUMBER	QUANTITY	PERSON WHO COLLECTED EVIDENCE:	WHERE EVIDENCE WAS DELIVERED TO:	DATE	TIME

ADDITIONAL CASE INFORMATION

Chain of custody form.

PHOTO LOG

Case # _____
Investigator _____

Date/Time	Photo #	Type Photo	Photo Depicts

Photo log.

Fingerprint 10-Print Card

NAME OF PERSON FINGERPRINTED (LAST, FIRST, MIDDLE)			DATE	
STREET ADDRESS	CITY		STATE	ZIP CODE
MALE/FEMALE	HEIGHT	WEIGHT	EYE COLOR	HAIR COLOR
DATE OF BIRTH	PLACE OF BIRTH (CITY AND STATE)			
SIGNATURE OF PERSON FINGERPRINTED		SIGNATURE OF PERSON TAKING FINGERPRINTS		

1	2	3	4	5
6	7	8	9	10

LEFT HAND	LEFT THUMB	RIGHT THUMB	RIGHT HAND

Fingerprint 10-print card.

Full Body: Female-Anterior and Posterior Views

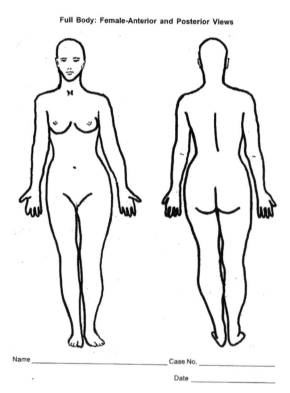

Name _____ Case No. _____

Date _____

Full Body: Male-Anterior and Posterior Views (Ventral and Dorsal)

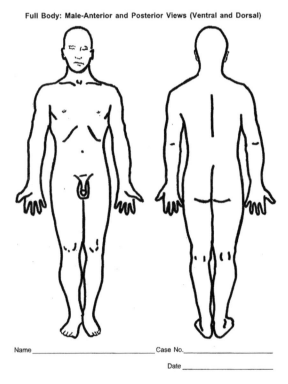

Name _____ Case No. _____

Date _____